An Insider's Guide to Johannesburg

J. M. Ostrowick

Editorial contact:

John Ostrowick
PO Box 150
WITS
2050
Johannesburg
Gauteng
South Africa
john@ostrowick.com

Copyright notices:

2nd Print Edition
© Aug 2, 2010 — John Ostrowick

All rights reserved. No part of the material protected by this copyright notice may be reproduced or utilised in any form, electronic or mechanical, including photocopying, recording, or by any information storage or retrieval system, without written permission from the copyright owner.

Cover design: John Ostrowick. All photography © J. M. Ostrowick with some exceptions courtesy of Wikimedia Commons, or cited websites.

ISBN 978-1-4457-4996-9

For the City of Gold.

Contents

Chapter	Page
1. Introduction	1
2. Politics and History	6
3. SA Culture	11
4. Useful information	18
5. Attractions with Historical Interest	30
6. Archaeological and Scientific Attractions	40
7. Shopping	44
8. Restaurants	48
9. Galleries	63
10. Nightlife — Bars, Nightclubs and Theatres	65
11. Sports	73
12. Theme Parks and Casinos	76
13. Animals, Game Parks and Nature Reserves	78
14. Accommodation	83
15. Maps	88

1

Introduction

Welcome to Johannesburg!

Johannesburg is severely underrated as a tourist destination. This could be because it has no beaches, no snow-capped mountains, and no ancient buildings — it is only about 124 years old. But Johannesburg has something else. Like New York, San Francisco, or any modern town that attracts large numbers of tourists, Johannesburg is a cultural and industrial centre, a place where people live and work. And like any place where people need to get away from their day-to-day routine, it has an enormous array of entertainment and cultural events running day and night to help people forget the humdrum of their daily lives.

Johannesburg has a massive immigrant population from all corners of the world; and as such, it is a cultural melting pot, anything but parochial.

In terms of night-life, Johannesburg has nightclubs and restaurants to serve every taste; whether you like R&B, jazz, hip-hop, pop, blues, rock, rave, heavy metal, goth, or world music, there's a nightclub that plays it as its chief fare. There are also many venues that feature live bands. You can sample the local African *Kwaito* beat (similar to rap, pronounced "**quite**-*oh*") or you can see a more western band playing hard rock. On the odd occasion there is an international act performing at one of the major amphitheatres. Or you can try some traditional Afrikaans *Sakkiemusiek* (a lot like American barn dance with a prominent accordion, pronounced "**suck**y-*miss*-**eek**").

The Soweto String Quartet

Johannesburg also occasionally features performances by the National Symphony Orchestra, and has at least five playhouses that put on various iconic productions.

2

Johannesburg is probably best-known by outsiders as the scene of the fall of the abominable Apartheid system, which kept millions of people oppressed for over four decades. The fall probably began with the Soweto Riots of 1976.

Shanty town in Soweto

Many of the city's occupants, as manual labourers, live in appalling conditions in shanty towns and squatter camps. Eddie Grant's song, "Give me hope Johanna," is about precisely this — the suffering of the people in the city under Apartheid, the effects of which have not yet dissipated. For this reason, if you're coming from a privileged country, a visit to Johannesburg is a worthwhile educational experience.

But Johannesburg is not just about Apartheid. For instance, the African Union Parliament sits in Midrand, just north of the city. And although Johannesburg is quite a young city, it has retained many Victorian-era leftovers. There are also some magnificent old colonial mansions and skyscrapers.

Furthermore, the human race evolved in the Johannesburg area; for this reason, it is called the "Cradle of Humankind". One can even argue that this area is the longest-inhabited place in the world; its history goes back at least two million years — longer than any other, except perhaps the Afar region in Ethiopia. The city is also the site of two major universities — The University of the Witwatersrand, also known as *Wits* (pronounced *Vits*), and University of Johannesburg. Wits runs all the archaeological digs.

Wits University

There are a number of game reserves very close to Johannesburg. There are also many museums, a large zoo, parks, theatres, live music and festivals.

Geographically, Johannesburg has many attractive natural features. It is split into bands running east-west by rows of *koppies* (rocky hills, Afrikaans: *small heads*, pronounced "***cor-peas***"), which offer superb views of the city. Some of these ridges were formed by ancient asteroid impacts.

The older suburbs are also so heavily planted with trees that it has been said that Johannesburg is the largest man-made forest. So the city has some very beautiful parts.

3

Johannesburg suburbs in mid-October.

Johannesburg is also the shopping capital of Africa. There are at least six major multi-storey shopping malls, plus a smaller mall in almost every suburb, and there are three or four major flea markets.

Bruma Flea Market

Most malls have the latest movies showing in their cinema sections, including 3D movies, but if you don't feel like going to a movie, you can always watch TV, as most good hotels are equipped with DSTV (digital satellite television), which consists of large numbers of predominantly US and UK channels.

As for food, whether you like Greek, Italian, Chinese, Japanese, Thai, German, Middle-Eastern, African, French, or just plain old pub or steakhouse food, there's a restaurant or two that will serve it in every major suburb.

Moyo African Restaurant at the Zoo Lake.

If you want to save money or time, you can just get fast food from one of the local or international franchises. If you're a vegetarian, you have nothing to worry about in Johannesburg — most restaurants, including fast-food places, support vegetarianism. If you are a carnivore, however, you should not leave South Africa without having gone to a *braai* (a barbeque, pronounced '*bri*' as in 'bright').

There are also many expositions that take place in Johannesburg, for example, Winex, which showcases the various wines from the Cape. You can't not know what is going on in Johannesburg, because every significant theatre production, entertainment offering, or exposition, is advertised extensively on billboards.

Summary

In summary, it is fair to say that Johannesburg is a city of strong contrasts; from corrugated iron shacks to massive skyscrapers, from street-children to multi-billionaires, from illiterate beggars to university professors. This is a town to see if you want to understand not only the recent history of South Africa, as well as humanity's primeval history, but also the great breadth of possibility with which humankind is endowed.

Statistics

Johannesburg is one of the largest cities on earth. It is a land-locked mass of buildings. It lies roughly 1500 km (932 miles) from Cape Town, and about 600 km from Durban.

Africa. South Africa is at the bottom.

Johannesburg occupies approximately as much area as London or New York, although, admittedly, it has fewer inhabitants than those metropolises, as it is more spread out. The inner city has a population of approximately 3.5 million people, but due to its sprawl, Johannesburg has absorbed most of the surrounding towns, bringing the population of the entire inhabited area of the province to 10 million people.

Provinces of SA. Note that Swaziland and Lesotho are independent nations. Cities marked are Cape Town (CPT), Johannesburg (JHB), and Durban (DBN)

Just to give you an idea of the size of the Johannesburg, if you drive the 70 km from the south of the city all the way to the (smaller) capital, Pretoria, which lies to the north, you will see very little open ground. The little province that houses Johannesburg, Pretoria, and their satellite towns, is called *Gauteng*; the Sotho word for gold. ("Gauteng" is pronounced, roughly, "*How-**teng**"*).

Johannesburg is not only immense, it is also the economic powerhouse of Africa, producing approximately one-third of South Africa's GDP, and approximately 10% of the entire continent's GDP. There are 53 nations in Africa, so it is not an exaggeration to say that the GDP of Johannesburg is equivalent to that of five African countries!

Johannesburg is affectionately known by a number of other names, such as *Jo'burg, Egoli* (the Zulu word for 'Place of Gold'), *The City of Gold,* and *Jozi.* It has also provided the name for the province of *Gauteng.* The reason is that Johannesburg's major industry, and indeed, the reason it was founded (in 1886), was and still is gold mining.

Old mining headgear

Most of South Africa's gold is mined in or around Johannesburg, and in the greater area called the *Witwatersrand,* or Gauteng. This former name means "white waters' ridge" in Afrikaans, a language derived from Dutch.

('*Witwatersrand*' is pronounced '*vert-**var**-terse-runt*'). The word refers to the colour of the Vaal river at the south border of Gauteng, and the geological ridge in which the gold is found. The "ridge" also gives its name to the South African currency, the Rand, which is divided up into 100 cents. The Rand is sometimes colloquially called the "buck", like the American currency, but unlike the latter, a one-Rand coin does actually have a buck on it.

South Africa is one of the world's largest producer of gold. Many giant companies were also founded in Johannesburg, for example: the brewing giant SABMiller (which owns many of the big breweries around the world), Anglo-American, and De Beers.

Jo'burg is thus not just an interesting place, it is also economically the most significant city on the continent.

Welcome and enjoy your stay!

Disclaimers

1. This book is not remotely exhaustive of all the options available in Johannesburg. It is just my personal list with my personal opinions.

2. Some of the tourist attractions that I have listed are not strictly inside Johannesburg. This is because they are quite easy to get to from Johannesburg, and are worth the trip.

3. Like all big cities, people in Johannesburg do experience crime. You should keep alert and avoid slummy areas, and people who seem to be loitering around for no good reason. I will not be held responsible for anything that may happen; you should get as much advice as you can on safety.

4. My coordinates are taken from Google Earth. I believe they are accurate but some may not be.

6

Chapter 2
Politics and History

Early History

In 1652, An exploration party led by a Hollander called Jan Van Riebeeck, arrived at the Cape.

The Post Office Stone

They established a post office and trading point there, and then later a fort (which still stands as the Cape Castle).
    The British arrived in the 1700s and decided that they wanted South Africa for its tactical position. The British settled in Cape Town (after conquering it), then in Durban, Port Elizabeth and East London in the early 1800s. The British rule was unpopular with the early Dutch settlers, for a variety of reasons, and compelled them to leave *en masse*. This was called the "Groot Trek" (literally the Great Drag or Great Move. 'Groot' is pronounced "**Hroo**-*it*").

Monument to the Battle of Blood River, showing the ox-wagon design

The Dutch packed up their belongings, and they moved inland, invading the seasonal grazing lands of the agrarian inhabitants. The Trekkers fenced off large areas of this land to set up farms, and called themselves the *Boers* (farmers). They engaged in wars with the people who saw the land as 'public' grazing. This created the racial tension that persists to this very day. When the British moved inland, the climate for all-out war was established. This conflict over land eventually culminated in the Anglo-Boer wars. Eventually the British won by pursuing a scorched-earth policy and interring the Dutch women and children into concentration camps, where they were maltreated, abused, and allowed to die of disease.

Boer women in a Concentration Camp.

The word "boor" comes from this war, as do many other loanwords such as "spoor", "veld" and "trek". The Dutch fought the British with a guerilla-war tactic, forcing the British to abandon their use of red uniforms. This war introduced guerilla war as the new face of warfare; previously, European wars had been fought with armies facing each other directly in lines. The British responded by adopting camouflaged uniforms and creating the Boy Scouts.

Baden-Powell, founder of the scouts.

Victorian Era and Early 20th Century

Gold was found in Johannesburg in 1886, reputedly by George Harrison (though some say it was his friend, George Walker), and diamonds were found in Kimberley. This sparked a new rush of British immigration.

In the early 20th century, under Jan Smuts, the British and Dutch agreed to disagree, creating the Union of South Africa, on 31 May 1910. ("Jan" — John — is pronounced "*Yun*").

Jan Smuts

This date was used as South Africa's Independence Day.

In the 1940s, the British Empire called the South Africans to war against Hitler in Egypt. When the primarily Afrikaans military returned, they found that the primarily English mining magnates had given their low-paid jobs to Africans, who were prepared to work harder, longer hours for less pay. This loss of employment resulted in what came to be known as the poor-white phenomenon. The white miners protested, and Smuts (who invented the psychological theory of Holism, and who apparently had a genius IQ), bombed the strikers with aircraft. This action made him unpopular with his previous supporters despite the fact that he encouraged the policy of segregation of the races. Resentment built and culminated in the defeat of Smuts' Unionist party by the primarily Afrikaans (Boer) Nationalist Party, called the "Nats", for short.

The old SA flag — combining the British Union Jack, the Boer Orange Free State flag, and the Boer Transvaal flag in the centre.

Apartheid Period

In 1948 the Nats deployed the Apartheid ("apartness") policy (it is pronounced **Apart**-hate, not Apart-*height*). Then, in 1956, the Nats implemented the Bantu Education policy (which taught Africans how to be servants). The Apartheid policy was sold as a "separate development" policy, but in fact it was effectively a land seizure and eviction policy, which ushered Africans into the poorest rural areas. It obliged them to carry passports in order to enter Apartheid South Africa, and stripped them of any rights when they were inside (these passports were called the 'dompas' or 'dumb pass' system, because they were despised).

All facilities, including park benches, buses, and public toilets, were segregated. Africans were only permitted menial jobs, and no-one was permitted to marry outside of their race. I recall that the Chinese were given some privileges, however, e.g., being allowed into white schools.

A sign on a beach during Apartheid

A policy of Christian National Education was introduced in the 1960s, in order to subjugate the Africans to the caretakership of the whites, on some Biblical justification. The government was also anti-semitic, and some members of the Nat government openly declared support for Hitler's racial ideologies. They also censored and banned any scientific work on evolution, because they felt that it undermined the Biblical basis of their racial policies, and threatened their church.

In 1961 the Nats negotiated independence from Britain and the Commonwealth, becoming the Republic of South Africa on 31 May 1961. In February 1962, they abandoned the Pound as the currency, replacing it with the Rand.

On June 16, 1976, the African township, Soweto, erupted into riot over enforced Afrikaans as the medium of education at schools. The riot was suppressed violently. Shortly after, the world's attention was drawn to South Africa, and the regime dug its heels in.

The ANC flag

In the 1980s, the international community imposed sanctions, which seemed to create sufficient pressure, combined with the liberation movement's terror activities (including civilian bombings), to cause the regime to relent.

De Klerk and Mandela

In 1990, Nelson Mandela, a purported "terrorist" and a leader of the ANC, was released from 27 years of imprisonment by the then State President, F. W. de Klerk. (The ANC was a left-wing pro-Socialism party. The name stands for "African National Congress.")

In 1994, Mandela became the first non-white president of South Africa, and Apartheid was dismantled. A progressive democratic constitution was put in place, which prohibited discrimination on all grounds, including race, gender, creed, and sexual orientation.

The PFP, who, up until that point had opposed the Nats in the white government, had to re-define their purpose. (The PFP was the original English-oriented party, the Progressive Federal Party). They renamed themselves to the DP (Democratic Party). The party subsequently allied itself with the Nats to create the DA (Democratic Alliance). The DA is still the official opposition party in parliament, but they now focus on keeping the government in check, particularly on issues around corruption.

The ANC currently holds about 67% of the vote, and thus remain the dominant power in the country. The DA is voted for primarily by whites (and in the Cape, coloureds tend to vote for them, too). The DA's official agenda is to become truly representative of all races and provide a credible alternative party to the ANC.

When Apartheid fell, a commission of enquiry was put in place. But instead of being a witch hunt like the Nuremburg Trials, it was intended as a healing process. It was called the Truth and Reconciliation Commission. It was headed by Archibishop Desmond Tutu, a former struggle activist and Anglican Bishop. He is still active today and acts as a credible African voice of opposition.

The new flag, introduced in 1994. It combines the colours of all the political parties that make up our rainbow nation.

Desmond Tutu

Chapter 3
SA Culture

Food and Drink

Food is probably one of the uniting features of South Africa. Apart from *Haute Cuisine*, South Africans pretty much enjoy the same kind of food — *braais* (barbeques — prounounced 'bri' as in 'bright'), and stews.

South African food is quite basic, and is oriented around meat and starch — *boerewors* (pronounced **boo**-*rer-vors*) and *mielies* (green corn on the cob, pronounced '***mee***-*lees*').

Boerewors in its packaging at the supermarket.

South Africans love beer — lager, specifically. And depending on their background, they might drink something called *Mageu* (pronounced '*muh-**HHey**o*') — a kind of fermented non-alcoholic maize derivative. They will also sometimes indulge in milk stout (fermented milk).

Wealthier South Africans, however, prefer wine, and often buy it in a cardboard box with a tap, so it can be dispensed conveniently and in large quantities at a *braai*. South Africa has been a wine farming country for centuries; in the 1600s, French Huguenots settled in the Cape, establishing the wine farms that still exist today. As a result, many Afrikaners (Dutch descendants), such as Charlize Theron, have French surnames. One of the things that wealthier South Africans do is drive the "Cape Wine Route". The scenery is mountainous, beautiful, and well worth it (please don't drive drunk).

Bobotie

Many South African dishes are of Cape Malay origin, e.g., Koeksisters ('***cook***-sisters', Lit.: cake-sisters) — a deep-fried, ginger syrup-steeped twisted doughnut, Bobotie ('*boo-**boor**-tee*') — a yellow-curried cottage pie with sultanas, baked with a thin savoury custard and bay leaf topping, and Sosaties ('*soo-**sar**-tees*') — spicy kebabs.

Other dishes are from the *Trekboers*. For example, *Melktert* (milktart, pronounced '***melk**-tat*' - but don't forget to roll the R) — this is a sweet, milky, creamy custard tart sprinkled with cinnamon, and served cold for tea. There is also *potjiekos* (Literally: small pot food, pronounced '***poy**-key-course*'), and *biltong:*

Potjiekos

Religion

Biltong is dried, spiced raw meat (usually beef or game). If you aren't a vegetarian, trying *biltong* or *droëwors* (dried sausage, pronounced '***droo**-er-vors*') is a mandatory part of the South African experience.

In the townships, you might enjoy a stew with *pap* (pronounced '*bub*') — a finely-milled stiff maize porridge, or some grilled chicken. Or perhaps you might be offered samp and beans — whole boiled maize kernels served like rice.

South Africa is quite a religious country, but there are constitutional checks in place which enforce tolerance, so although the country has a Christian majority, no-one may legally enforce any particular religion, especially in schools. Our Constitution has given us total division of Church and State. We do not have a national religion and we do not have religious ceremonies on State occasions such as the Inauguration of the President. Instead of a prayer or a Bible reading, the incoming president is hailed by a traditional praise-singer ("*imbongi*"). Stats SA reports that the metropolis, Johannesburg, is about 76% Christian. Islam is quite prominent in Johannesburg and Cape Town, and Hinduism is most common in Durban, on the east coast. The Zulus have an African tribal church which borrows elements from Christianity and traditional beliefs, called Zulu Zion, and there is a new, similar system which focuses on a latter-day prophet, Shembe. Each tribe has its own beliefs and systems, but the majority of

Africans practice some variant on, or variety of, Christianity.

Sport

South Africans are very much an outdoors-oriented bunch. The majority are involved in, or interested in, some sort of outdoor sports. Richer people tend to favour golf, racing bicycles, gym, climbing. Afrikaners and English alike tend to devoutly follow two British sports: rugby and cricket. The rest of the country tends, in the vast majority, to follow mainly soccer (football).
    Basketball, American Football and baseball are not followed in SA.

In the eyes of most South Africans, a great weekend consists of turning on the TV to watch sport, while darting in and out of the house to check on the braai.

Music

South African music tends to be divided along racial lines. There are a number of local music types, for example, *Kwaito* (a kind of rap in an African language), and gospel music, particularly sung in an African language.

More intellectual people tend to go for jazz (preferably local), and the upper classes occasionally indulge in the National Symphony Orchestra.

There are some crossover bands which sing primarily in English, with an African sound, e.g., Johnny Clegg, but they're not that common.

Most South African bands play either Jazz, Kwaito, or some kind of hard rock. In fact the band Seether (formerly known as Saran Gas) did grunge so well that they met with greater success in the USA and moved there. The same applies to Dave Matthews, who also came from South Africa.

The South African club scene is split along music genre lines; most places play local African music and Rap or R&B. Some play House or Rave, but there are a few exceptions here and there that play rock or pop.

There are dozens of radio stations, catering to every taste. You can just turn the dial and decide on what you like. Almost all stations play African music of some kind, so you're most likely to hear that. But there are at least three stations that play pop music from the USA and UK.

South African English

South Africa is home to *eleven* official languages — as well as a large number of unofficial ones. There is even a specific form of sign language used for the deaf, and another very specific sign language used in hailing minibus taxis.

Because of Apartheid, which pushed the Afrikaners and English into the same camp, English in South Africa has been most heavily influenced by Afrikaans.

The South African accent is a bit flat, e.g., "tin" is pronounced more like "tern". Similarly, diphthongs are often flattened to "ah," so the words "high," "ha" and "how" all sound alike — "hah."

South African English speakers do, however, pride themselves in following British spelling and word usage.

If you want to learn more about South Africa's fascinating variety of languages, simply go into any branch of Exclusive Books, and look in the language section for a book on the language that you'd like to learn.

The eleven official languages are: *Afrikaans, English, IsiNdebele (Ndebele), IsiXhosa (Xhosa), IsiZulu (Zulu), Sepedi (Pedi), Sesotho (Sotho), Setswana (Tswana), SiSwati (Swazi), Tshivenda (Venda), Xitsonga (Tsonga).* Zulu and Xhosa are the biggest.

15

SA English Vocabulary

The following word list is a small selection of odd words and unusual usages that you will quite likely encounter during your time in South Africa.

Word	Meaning
Howzit (pronounced **Haa**zit)	Hi. (*Lit.*: How is it). Not a question, it is a greeting. Best response is "Ja, Howzit." South Africans do also use *Hi* and *Hey* as greetings; but *howzit* is a more macho greeting. Stick to "Hi" if you're not sure. If someone says "Howzit hey?" *then* you are being asked how you are. The answer is "No I'm fine ".
Ja (pronounced like *yar* — but don't pronounce the R)	Yes. (Casual). Direct from Afrikaans. Can start a sentence to denote acknowledgement, e.g., "Ja, no OK." Used the same as UK/USA "Yeah".
Robot	Traffic lights.
Now, now-now, just now	Actually means "when I get around to it." Not considered to be rude. "Right now" is probably the only usage of "now" that means "at this very instant".
No	Means *no*, or the start of a spoken reply. E.g., "Howzit hey?" "No I'm fine ."
Ja-no, Ja-nee (**yar**-*near* — but don't pronounce the Rs)	An expression of uncertainty or ironic amusement. Literally yes-no. From Afrikaans.
Sorry	"Pardon?", but also used if you wish to express empathy, even when it's not your fault, e.g., if you see someone trip.
Check	See, look at, watch. As in, "Did you check the rugby hey?"
Oke, ou (*oh*)	Bloke. Chap. Guy. From Afrikaans "ou", perhaps the phrase "ou kêrel" (old chap, pronounced "Oh Carol"). E.g., "Check that oke" means "Look at that guy!"
Ag (*uhHH*)	Same as German *ach*. An expression of exasperation or disgust.
Man!	An exclamation of annoyance, e.g., "Ag, man!" This results in humorous turns of phrase like, "Ag lady, man! Don't do that!"

16

Word	Meaning
Lekker (***lack***er)	Very nice, tasty, sweet. Afrikaans. Also used to express *schadenfreude*, e.g., "Lekker! Serve him right!"
Sies, sis (*seess, serss*)	An exclamation of disgust, usually at dirt or lewdness.
Cheers	Means goodbye or a salutation over drinks only, not thanks (as in the UK).
Jol (*djorl* — but don't pronounce the R)	To have a fun time (*n*), to play (*v*). E.g., "Do you want to jol rugby? It will be a jol!"
Shame	Means shame, pity, empathy, or even admiration for something cute.
Coloured	A person of mixed race (only).
Chips	Deep fried potato chips (hot) *or* potato crisp snacks (cold). *Slaptjips* or *Slapchips* (pronounced **slup**-chips) are sloppy chips — an SA favourite: thick, oily, sloppy, deep-fried potato chips.
Lapa (***lah***-pah)	A thatched gazebo. In Zulu, however, *lapha* (pronounced the same) means "there".
Stoep (*stoop*)	Verandah. Afrikaans, but used in English.
Braai (*bry*)	A barbeque. Afrikaans.
Pap (*bub, pup*)	Stiff porridge made from white maize. Eaten savoury at a *braai*, usually with tomato and onion ratatouille. Afrikaans. Similar to polenta, but more finely milled.
Mielie (***mee***-lee)	Corn, usually white, i.e., usually not sweet-corn, usually on the cob. Maize. A staple of the SA diet, most often *braai*ed.
Biltong (***berl***-torng — but don't pronounce the Rs)	Beef jerky. Dried, spiced raw meat. National favourite snack.
Bakkie (***buck***ie)	A pickup truck. From Afrikaans, meaning a small container. Can also refer to all flattish containers, e.g. Tupperware. Compare to English "bucket."
Takkies (***teck***ies, ***tack***ies)	Running shoes. Sneakers.
Veld (*felt*)	Grasslands. Note the pronunciation.

17

Word	Meaning
Bundu-bashing	Hiking through the veld or jungle.
Koppie (**corpie** — but don't pronounce the R.*)*	A rocky hill.
Shebeen	An informal and formerly illegal tavern.
Township, location	A formerly black-only area, usually poor and crowded, with poor infrastructure. A relic of the Apartheid regime.
Tsotsi (**tsor**-*tsee*)	A gangster or thug.
Is it? Is it hey?	Really? You reckon? Note that "Is it hey?" is more of an irritated response, e.g., compare "The springboks just lost" "Oh, is it?" versus "The springboks are a lousy side" "Is it hey?"
Klap (*clup*)	To smack or hit. E.g. "The springboks are a lousy side" may receive a response "You looking for a *klap*?" (Afrikaans).

There are many more terms you will hear in use in South Africa. This is not remotely an exhaustive list, and it's only the words used by English speakers. As there are more than eleven other languages, don't be surprised by the enormous variety of words you will hear, and that there will be other words not on this list.

Samples of other languages in Johannesburg

The pronunciation of the words listed here is tricky, so listen first. For example, C, Q and X are all clicks in the African languages, TH is always a T, K is a G, HL is fricative, and so on.

Hello/Good Morning/Day — Hallo, Gooie Môre/Dag (Afrikaans, pronounced **Hwee**-*a*-**more**-*er* or **Hwee**-*a*-**duHH**) — Sawubona (singular)/Sanibonani (plural) (Zulu, pronounced **Sow**-*oo*-**born**-*a* and **Sun**-*bore*-**nun**) — Molo (sing.)/Molweni (plur.) (Xhosa) — Unjani? (How are you — Zulu and Xhosa, pronounced *oon*-**djahn**). You'll notice that Africans always ask after your health. Dumela (sing.) Dumelang (plur., pronounced *Doo*-**mel**-*a*) /Mmoro (Sesotho). O/Le kae? (How are you?, pronounced *lair*-**guy**) Sesotho. Setswana and Sepedi are similar to Sesotho and the greetings are the same. **Goodbye.** Sala Kahle/Hamba Kahle (Zulu, pronounced **hum**-*bah*-**gush**-*lair*). Sala hantle (Sesotho). Totsiens (Afrikaans, pronounced **tort**-*seenss*, literally meaning 'until see').

18

Chapter 4
Useful Information

Weather

The weather in South Africa is generally excellent. Winters seldom go below 10°C (except at night, when they can go down to -2°C), and summers seldom exceed 35°C, usually hovering in the upper 20s. Most days are wind-free, rain-free, and warm, around 25°C. In winter, South Africa's day temperatures tend to be around 10-15°C, with clear deep blue skies in most parts of the country. The Western Cape and Cape Town, however, often experience light rain, drizzle and wind in winter.

You must be advised that most buildings in South Africa are not double-glazed and do not have central heating, so winters can be cold and unpleasant if you come unprepared, especially in Johannesburg, which can get snow on some rare occasions.

That's about as much snow as we get.

If you're visiting in winter (May-August), make sure you bring warm clothes, especially for night-time.

The daylight hours are more-or-less the same throughout the seasons; sunrise is usually around 5 AM (Summer)/7 AM (Winter) and sunset is usually around 7 PM (Summer)/5 PM (Winter). However, Cape Town sunset in summer is around 9 PM.

A typical afternoon storm brewing.

In the late afternoons in summer on the highveld (high plains in the interior, where Johannesburg sits), South Africa often experiences dramatic thunderstorms. Occasionally, there is a week or so of overcast weather, but it's quite rare for clouds to persist for more than a week. You could hardly ask for a better climate.

Sunset over Johannesburg

Johannesburg is about 1750m above sea-level. The air is, consequently, thin and dry. It can also be smoggy in parts, especially the city centre. Asthmatics should bring their medicines.

Tipping, Buying Power and Exchange Rate

South Africa has many part-time workers who earn very little, so it is considered very mean to not tip. It is customary to tip waiters, barkeepers, car guards, tour guides, and petrol pump attendants. The accepted tipping rate for waiters is 10%. Barkeepers are usually grateful for anything silver. Car guards should be paid between R 2 and R 5, but not less. If the car guard washed your car (usually at a cost of about R 30), you should add the guarding tip to the cost of washing the car. Tour guides see themselves as specialists, so tipping less than R 10 is probably an insult; R 20 is probably safer. Most people give petrol pump attendants R 2 to R 5.
    You might want to consider keeping a small cache of coins in your car for parking attendants (who are casual workers who try to prevent car theft), and beggars at the traffic intersections.

Money

The South African currency is the Rand, divided into 100 cents. Your ATM (cash machine) card, debit card, or credit card, should work just fine in South Africa. Most shops only take VISA/MasterCard, however.

Just so that you understand the buying power of the Rand, it is approximately $1/10$ of one British Pound for the same product. A restaurant meal for one person typically costs around R 100-150, including drinks, but can be as little as R 50. This translates to about £ 5-15. Of course, this varies as the exchange rate varies. There are forex offices at most airports and in most malls. I recommend against using traveller's cheques, however, as I do not know of many shops that accept them. The petrol price also varies quite dramatically at the government's whim.

Internet Access

South Africa has the best internet connectivity in Sub-Saharan Africa. We have 3G, GPRS, and WiFi in most major cities, as well as ADSL/DSL. If you are likely to need internet access, please check that your accommodation offers it first, as you may experience difficulty obtaining GPRS/3G coverage, for reasons explained below.

There are many places that offer WiFi or use of computer terminals, especially in malls, so you're unlikely to be unable to get internet access. Be aware that you should never give your banking details over internet in a public place such as a hotel or internet café.

Telephony

South Africans love their cellular telephones. In fact, almost everyone has one, from the richest to the poorest. Our network is GSM-based, so American visitors should ensure that their cellphones are GSM-capable, i.e., quad- or tri-band. There are not many public telephones and a large proportion of them take special cards that you have to purchase at stores, rather than coins. So you probably need a working cellphone, especially in case you get lost.

South Africa recently introduced an anti-terrorism and anti-crime law which requires all cellphone holders to register their cellphones at a cellphone store. This law is called RICA. The trouble is, you're required to bring ID and proof of residence. I am not sure that a hotel booking sheet or foreign passport will suffice; in my experience, most cellphone stores want or expect South African proof of residency, and will refuse to sell you a phone or SIM-card unless you can do so. So it is crucial that before you leave your home country, that you ensure that your cellular service provider has a roaming agreement with one of the South African service providers, so that your phone will continue to work when you land. If this is not possible, you can ask for advice from your own service provider.

If you manage to purchase a SIM-card in South Africa, you can top up your airtime or talking minutes at most ATMs or shops.

There are presently seven telephone network operators in South Africa: Vodacom, Telkom, Telkom Mobile (8•ta), MTN, Virgin, Cell C, and Neotel. Vodacom and MTN own the cellphone signal masts, so they probably will give you the best signal, but Virgin is probably the cheapest.

Electricity

Left: British, Right: South African

South Africa uses 220 VAC, 50-60 Hz. You will need to buy an adapter when you land at the airport. Make sure that if you are coming from an area that uses 110 volts that your devices have switching power supplies.

Water

All houses and rooms in the tourist areas are equipped with running water and normal toilet facilities. If you require an Islamic toilet, you may have to plan in advance and find an establishment which has these.

Tap water in South Africa is completely safe to drink. River or dam water is not.

Transport

Introduction

South Africa is a very car-oriented country as the public transport systems are relatively poor. Johannesburg is far too big to walk. Minibus taxis drive poorly. Municipal buses are safer but their routes are very limited. There is a new train service called the *Gautrain*, intended for use by foreign visitors coming from the main airport, Oliver Tambo, but its route is limited, so you can't rely on it for everything.

You can arrange transport with taxi cabs (in South Africa, the word 'taxi' usually means a minibus taxi). But taxi cabs are very expensive in South Africa, so it makes much more sense to hire a car at the airport.

If you get lost

I recommend that if you get lost, that you should look for the blue motorway signs, and stay on the M1 or N12/N3. On the N3/N12 ring road, there are certain exits you should avoid. Local people can advise you on this. You should also try to get a car with a GPS. I have included some basic maps in this book, but they will not suffice.

Rules, Signs and Speeds

South Africans drive on the left (as in the UK), and the road signs are generally the same. Most importantly, tourist signs are brown and motorway signs are blue. If you see a small green or blue sign with a number on it, followed by (N, S, E, W), that is a *route marker* and it tells you what route you're on, and what direction you're travelling in.

Some roadsigns in South Africa are still in Afrikaans. As a result, you may find some road names confusing. For example, you might be looking for a road called Smith Road, and your GPS says you're at Smith Road, but the sign says *Smithweg*. To help you with this confusion, please be aware that "weg" is "road" ('way', literally), "str" or "straat" is "street", "ryln" or "rylaan" are "drive" (literally 'ridelane'), and "laan" or "ln" means "avenue", (but is literally 'lane'). Unlike the UK, we use "lane" as just another word for "road", it doesn't specifically mean a cul-de-sac or side road from a main road.

Our speeds are measured in metric units: Kilometres per hour (km/h). In case you don't have a convenient converter available, one metre is roughly a yard, and one kilometer is 1000 metres, or 0.62 miles. The urban speed limit is 60 km/h (37mph), large roads: 80 km/h (50mph), motorways: 120 km/h (75mph). The fines for exceeding the speed limits are severe, and the speed traps are deliberately hidden and are usually manned by police officers. Many traffic lights also

22

have traps on them so that if you jump through the light after it's turned orange, you will get a fine.

Choosing your car at the airport

Almost all cars in SA have a manual transmission, but you should be able to get an automatic in Johannesburg; in other cities it's less likely. You will be offered insurance on your car at the airport. I strongly recommend that you take comprehensive insurance. I also strongly recommend that you get a car with an air conditioner. You should also not choose a luxury sedan that is likely to be targeted by criminals. Don't forget to check your car thoroughly for chips or dents before you leave the airport, otherwise you will pay for them when you return the car.

Parking

There is usually plenty of parking in South African cities. Most street parking is free, so don't worry about parking meters unless you see one. Sometimes car guards will offer to feed the meter for you if there is a meter, e.g., outside the Civic Theatre. Let them do so. You will always have to pay to park in a mall, but most malls allow you fifteen minutes' grace to drop off passengers.

Note, however, that unlike the UK, you may not park facing the traffic, and you may not park on a solid painted line. You may only park in designated parking areas. If in doubt, do what the locals are doing.

Laws

All passengers in a moving vehicle must wear seat belts.

Cellphone use by a driver is prohibited.

The legal blood alcohol limit is two beers or one glass of wine. Realistically speaking, this is probably too much.

Traffic police typically look for speeding or driver's licenses during the day and drunk driving at night.

Any driver's license should be acceptable, but in practice the traffic police have been known to demand international licenses, which you can get at your local branch of the Automobile Association.

Traffic police wear brown and blue uniforms and drive orange and white cars.

The regular police (who deal with crimes) wear blue uniforms and drive white vehicles.

Be careful of politicians when on the roads; they drive black luxury vehicles with blue lights and they tend to push you out the way. It's best if you stay in the middle or left lane on a motorway as the politicians and SUV drivers are quite rude. You will notice that minibus taxis (and others) drive in the yellow (emergency) lane. Do not do this, it is illegal.

Avoiding Traffic Jams

Traffic in Johannesburg is very heavy. There is always a traffic jam on the run to Midrand, Sandton and the airport. It's generally a better bet, if you're pressed for time, to go through the suburbs. Do not assume that you can get from your departure point to your destination in less than an hour.

In particular, the traffic to the airport is always heavy at all times of day and night, so you should allocate yourself two hours before check-in time to get to the airport if you're going by car. (Or just catch the Gautrain instead). If you know that there's a traffic jam on the way to the airport (e.g. because you heard it on the radio), it's often a good idea to drive through Edenvale and Sebenza and take the Barbara Road offramp onto the R24, left. At least that will help you to avoid most of the motorway.

The airport, taken from the air

Rush hour (or rather, rush-three-hours) is typically 6.30 AM to 10 AM, and 3.30 PM to 6.30 PM. In other words, if you're planning a day out, you should leave your hotel later in the morning, and return in the earlier part of the afternoon, 9 AM to 3 PM, say.

Safety

It is worth mentioning that pedestrians quite often run across the roads, including motorways! Keep a keen eye out for pedestrians, especially at night on the M2 south and N3/N12 east side motorway running between the airport and Sandton/Midrand.

Many accidents occur when it is raining, as the rain in Jo'burg is heavy and it is hard to see ahead of you. The rain usually appears around 3 PM in summer.

South Africans have a custom of flashing their lights. If the traffic is coming towards you, it is to warn you of danger up ahead, that there are police ahead, or they're telling you to dim your lights. South Africans also turn on their emergency lights when stopping or slowing down abruptly. If someone flashes their lights behind you, it usually means "get out of the way". Legally, this rudeness is allowed in the right-hand lane on a motorway. Sometimes the person behind you might flash you once. This usually happens if they let you into their lane; it means "Say thanks!" or "My pleasure!" To say thanks to someone when you cut into a lane, either raise your hand or blink your emergency lights twice.

You may also notice that Johannesburgers sometimes fail to indicate before turning, especially if cutting into your lane. Stay alert and anticipate this behaviour. Watch out for taxis (minibuses). They can and will do anything illegal, including cutting ahead of you from a turning lane, driving on pavements, driving into oncoming traffic, etc.

Filling Up

Petrol stations are attended by staff, so you are expected to not fill up yourself. You should ask the attendant to "fill up, to automatic stop," otherwise he will try to squeeze as much petrol as possible into your tank. Or you can ask for a specific amount in Rands. Most car tanks are about 43 litres, so expect to pay about R 300 - R 400. A tank should get you about 500-800 km. This estimate is based on a standard 43 L tank (11 US Gallons). Do not be fooled. Johannesburg is very big, and it is easy to do 100 km in one day, just on daily errands, so a tank will usually only last a week.

Petrol pump attendants will also offer you other services such as checking oil, water, tyre pressure, and cleaning your windscreen. If they do

24

these additional services, it is considered appropriate to tip them. In fact, it is usual to tip them a few Rands just for dispensing the petrol, too. Tyre pressure is measured in atmospheres or *bars* ("Two bar all round" is the phrase).

Because of the very common occurrence of traffic jams in Johannesburg, you should make sure that you always have a quarter of a tank of petrol; don't let it go below that.

Airports

Johannesburg has four airports — Oliver Tambo (formerly Johannesburg International), Lanseria, Rand, and Grand Central. All of them are very small except Oliver Tambo, which is very large (The grounds are 7km x 4km in size!). The other airports are mainly for internal flights. OR Tambo airport is in Kempton Park on the East Rand (Ekurhuleni). Coordinates are: 26° 7'57.50"S, 28°13'39.48"E.

Health and Safety

Johannesburg has many large (and free) public hospitals, but they have poor facilities, and the queues are long. If you have the time, rather look for the private "Medicross" clinics or other private hospitals such as Netcare. Medicross clinics tend to be geared towards minor problems only.

Netcare Hospitals (*www.netcare.co.za*) may require payment up-front, and may decline to treat you if your medical aid or health insurance provider offers any obstacles (This up-front payment may be as much as R 10 000, so make sure you have about £ 1000 in your credit card!

The emergency services telephone numbers are:

112 and 999.

Johannesburg's general phone number for traffic problems and emergencies is:

+27-11-375-5555,

or, if you're on a local phone,

011-375-5555.

Police: 10111

If the treatment comes to less than R 10 000 they will refund the difference. Never fear, a doctor's consultation is "only" R200 or so). There is also the Mediclinic group: *www.mediclinic.co.za*. There are dozens of hospitals and clinics around Johannesburg, however, these are some of the major ones that are located in the central Johannesburg area (inside the N1/N3/N12 ring road):

Private Hospitals

Central Sandton: Morningside Medi-clinic
Phone: +27 11 282 5000
Address: Hill Road, Morningside
Coordinates: 26° 5'38.62"S
28° 3'17.33"E

North-west: Sandton Clinic
Phone: +27 11 709 2000
Address: Cnr Braam Fischer (formerly HF Verwoerd) and Peter Place, Randburg

Coordinates: 26° 4'39.17"S
28° 0'43.41"E

North: Netcare Sunninghill
Phone: +27 11 806 1500
Address: Cnr Nanyuki & Witkoppen Roads, Sunninghill
Coordinates: 26° 2'14.66"S
28° 4'9.96"E

Central/East: Netcare Linksfield
Phone: +27 11 647 3400
Address: 24 12th Avenue, Orange Grove/Linksfield
Coordinates: 26° 9'35.62"S
28° 5'42.69"E

Netcare Milpark
Phone: +27 11 480 5600
Address: Guild Street, off Empire Road, Parktown
Coordinates: 26°10'50.75"S
28° 1'6.02"E

Public Hospitals

Central: Johannesburg General Hospital
Phone: +27 11 488 4911
Address: Jubilee Rd, Parktown
Web: www.johannesburghospital.org.za
Coordinates: 26°10'36.29"S, 28° 2'41.95"E

East: Edenvale Hospital
Phone: +27 11 321 6000
Address: Modderfontein Road, Sandringham/Edenvale
Coordinates: 26° 7'41.62"S,
28° 7'43.17"E

Medicines

You should bring all the medicines that you require with you, as well as a script or prescription from your doctor saying what drugs you normally require and what conditions you have. Medicines can be quite costly, and you should ask for the "generic" of the drug. Drugs have to be paid for immediately. You can purchase drugs directly from a chemist without a prescription as long as the drug required is lower than Schedule-3. If you have asthma or allergies, or bites or stings, there are plenty of Schedule-2 drugs that you can get over the counter without a doctor's script.

Dangerous animals

Regarding bites and stings, you must expect that South Africa's hospitable climate encourages the proliferation of potentially dangerous creatures. The African **bees**, for example, are very aggressive and often pollinate flowers on the lawns, so you are advised to walk with shoes on and keep away from bees. Pour your soda (or as we call it, your 'cooldrink'), into a glass in case a bee lands inside the can.

I've never seen a **snake** in Johannesburg and most are not harmful, but all snakes should be treated with extreme caution. If you are bitten, seek medical attention immediately; do not delay, as some bites can be lethal, e.g., adders' bites.

A puff adder or 'pofadder'

South Africa also has a range of **button spiders**, related to the Black Widow, all of which are dangerous and very common in cities. You can recognise them by their proportionally large abdomen. They are usually brown or black and about 1-2cm (0.5"-1") in size when fully grown. See the following images so that you can identify them.

Other spiders, especially ones that do not sit in webs, are not generally dangerous, but *all* spiders and snakes should be treated with *extreme* caution.

Pictures courtesy of spiderwatch.za.org

South Africa also has a lot of **mosquitos** in summer. Fortunately, only the mosquitos in the north-east of the country carry malaria, so you probably do not need to take malaria tablets unless you're going to the Kruger National Park or Northern KwaZulu-Natal. Do not go to these areas if you are pregnant. Bring mosquito repellant. If you are bitten, I recommend *Anthisan* cream, available at all chemists.

Be careful when hiking in long grass as you may pick up **ticks**. If you are bitten by a tick, you may get *tickbite fever*, which is very serious. Wear long pants. Also check your hiking boots for bugs before putting them on.

HIV/AIDS

South Africa has a very high incidence of HIV/AIDS: up to 33% in females in their late 20s. The population average is 10%. You are advised strongly to use a condom. *http://www.hsrc.ac.za/Factsheet-40.phtml.*

Crime

South African cities have a reputation for crime. Unfortunately, we have many poor and desperate people. The key to avoiding any unpleasant experiences is to use your common sense.
Crime in South Africa is almost entirely opportunistic in nature. Avoid carrying anything of value in a showy manner, including cameras.

If you're touring an area that looks dirty, abandoned or slummy, make sure you're in a large group. Keep away from loiterers, and keep alert. If you are confronted, keep your eyes lowered as a sign of respect, to avoid provocation.

Tourist attractions, malls, restaurants, and other entertainment venues are not often targeted by criminals, but it is wise to be vigilant around banking areas, as some banks and ATMs in malls have been robbed. Do not accept help from strangers at ATMs (cash machines), as the person may be a con artist.

The easiest way to avoid being harassed is to drive everywhere (rather than walk), and keep your valuables out of sight, except in a restaurant, mall or cinema, where you *must* keep them on your lap or in front of you. Do not wear your bag on your back. Do not leave valuables unattended at any time. Keep items in the safe at the hotel where possible.

Specific safety advice:

• *Car hijacking* — This is the forced seizure of your car. It can happen in abandoned areas (e.g. at night) or just outside the place you're staying, once you're trapped in the driveway. If you see loiterers, phone the the hotel to have them removed. If you think another car is following you, go straight to the police. Hijackers tend to favour luxury vehicles, pickup trucks and old Toyotas (so hire something obscure at the airport like Saab, Volvo, etc.). Do not argue with hijackers under any circumstances, just hand over the car.

• *Smash and grab* — criminals may smash your car window at the traffic lights and take whatever they can see.

• *Car theft* — if you leave your car unlocked or in a back alley or other abandoned place, it is likely to be stolen or robbed. Always park where there are other cars, lots of people, and car guards, or somewhere that you can see your car. It is best to park in a mall, as the security is tighter. Avoid parking in side roads.

Police Stations

Assuming that you're staying in the Rosebank/Sandton area, these are the police stations in that area:

Rosebank
Address: Cnr Keyes Ave & 7th Ave
Coordinates: 26° 8'43.03"S
28° 2'13.01"E

Phone : +27 11 778 4700
Address : 15 Sturdee Ave
Coordinates: 26° 8'42.00"S
28° 2'18.83"E

Sandton
Phone: +27 11 615 5537
Address: 25 Cleveland Rd, Sandhurst
Coordinates: 26° 6'58.29"S
28° 2'14.88"E (approximate)

Phone: +27 11 722 4355 / 4200
Address: 2 Summit Rd Dunkeld West
Coordinates: 26° 7'41.28"S
28° 1'56.94"E (approximate)

There are probably in the region of 100 police stations scattered around the city. Your GPS or map book should show them.

Smoking and Drinking in Public

You may generally smoke out-of-doors, away from the doorways, or in a private house or its garden, or inside a restaurant's designated smoking area, or in a park. Other than that, you should assume that you may not smoke. You should be especially careful of smoking in game parks and protected areas. This has caused some fires and substantial damage, resulting in destruction of valuable natural resources, the deaths of rare animals, and enormous fines for the offender. *Never toss your cigarette butt out of your car window;* South Africa generally has large areas of dry grass fields ("veld" — pronounced "felt") next to the road, and it catches fire easily, especially in winter (May-August).

You are advised not to smoke in rented cars as you may be liable for any damage to the vehicle. It is illegal to smoke in a car with children.

You may only drink in a restaurant, nightclub, bar, or private home. You may not consume alcohol in the street, or in a mall's corridor, or in a park or on a beach (without permission), or on public transport, or whilst driving. Venue proprietors have the right to evict persons who are inebriated and refuse to serve them.

All recreational drugs are illegal in South Africa and the penalties for dealing, or possessing large quantities, are severe.

Public Holidays in SA in 2010

1 January	New Year's Day
21 March	Human Rights Day
2 April	Good Friday
5 April	Family Day
27 April	Freedom Day
1 May	Workers Day
16 June	Youth Day
9 August	Women's Day
24 September	Heritage Day
16 December	Day of Reconciliation
25 December	Christmas Day
26 December	Day of Goodwill

South Africa has quite a few public holidays. Generally, only shops and entertainment venues operate on public holidays or Sundays. Christmas is the exception; almost everything is shut on 25 December.

Note that if a holiday falls on a weekend, then the subsequent Monday will be a holiday. Also note that since the date of Easter changes every year, the dates given below apply only in 2010.

A brief note on the meaning behind some of these holidays: March 21 commemorates the Sharpeville massacre. April 27 is the day Mandela was released from prison. June 16 is the date of the Soweto Riots, when schoolchildren were killed. December 16 was a day celebrated by the

Afrikaners in honour of a vow made to God during the Zulu war, that if they won, they would hold the day sacred. Because that holiday was considered racist, it has been renamed to "Day of Reconciliation". On December 26, also known as "Boxing Day", it is customary to give a "Christmas Box" to cleaners, garbage removal men, and beggars — usually money, but any gift is acceptable.

Office Hours

Most businesses run from 8 AM to 5 PM on workdays, or 9 AM to 1 PM on Saturdays, but it varies from company to company. Some companies run training from 8 AM to 9 AM on Wednesdays. Most shops only open at 9 - 9.30 AM and close at 5 PM. Banks usually work shorter hours on a Saturday. Food and entertainment industries typically operate until 11 PM, except bars and clubs, which can run as late as 4 AM.

Grocery stores in malls generally run from 9 AM to 6 PM. Spar, in particular, stays open until 7 or 8 PM. There are no 24-hour grocery stores. Some fast-food chains are open 24 hours, but they are rare; most close at 11 PM.

Garages (petrol stations), and hospital emergency wards, are mostly open 24/7. Most garages have convenience stores that are open 24/7.

It is worth noting that one mall in particular in Johannesburg — the Oriental Plaza — observes Muslim prayer times on Friday, around 12 noon. More information on this mall is available in the chapter on shopping.

Taxi Cabs

You're advised to hire a car instead of relying on costly taxi cabs. If, however, you're going out drinking, hire a cab. "It's cheaper than bail," as the saying goes.

- www.sacab.co.za — 08611 72222
- www.londoncabs.co.za — 0861 11 4966
- www.mrshuttle.co.za (airport transfers) — 082 800 5788
- www.bradcorp.co.za — 011 023 6668
- www.rosetaxis.com (the longest-running taxi company, dating back to 1934) — 011 403 0000 / 403 9625

Chapter 5
Attractions with Historical Interest

Introduction

Now that I've covered the background about South Africa, and Johannesburg in particular, let's take a look at some of the tourist attractions that you might want to see in our great city, starting with attractions of recent historical or political interest. This chapter does not cover primeval history or attractions dealing with human evolution; for this, see the later chapter on scientific interest.

In some cases, I have listed things to see in Pretoria. This is because Pretoria is easy to get to from Johannesburg and contains many attractions of great historical import.

In Johannesburg Itself

The Apartheid Museum — This museum, built after the fall of Apartheid, showcases the excesses of the Apartheid regime. It is the premier tourist destination of Johannesburg. Some displays are not suitable for young children.

Phone: +27 11 309 4700
Address: Cnr Northern Parkway and Gold Reef Road, Ormonde
Web: www.apartheidmuseum.org
Coordinates: 26°14'16.53"S 28° 0'38.54"E

Constitutional Court, The Old Fort and Women's Jail — On the ridge between Hillbrow and Braamfontein in central Johannesburg, we find the modern Constitutional Court building, and the old Fort and Women's Jail, which has housed a great number of very famous prisoners, including Mahatma Gandhi and Nelson Mandela.

It is recommended that you take a guided tour so as to not miss out on all the personal snippets about the various prisoners and the history of the place.

Phone: +27 11 274 5300, +27 11 381 3100

Address: Joubert Street Extension, Braampark
Web: www.constitutionhill.org.za
Coordinates: 26°11'15.73"S
28° 2'32.64"E

Gandhi as a lawyer in South Africa

The Cooling Towers — These cooling towers, a landmark in Soweto, used to power the city during Apartheid, but have been decommissioned and painted with murals. Apparently one can bungee jump off them!

Address: Nicholas Street, Diepkloof/Power Park
Coordinates: 26°15'15.35"S,
27°55'35.00"E

George Harrison Statue — A statue of George Harrison, who discovered gold in the Johannesburg area in 1886, effectively founding the city. Located at the entrance to the Johannesburg municipality coming from the eastern highway from the airport, at Eastgate Shopping Mall.

I'd say it's only worth a look if you happen to be going to Eastgate or Bruma Fleamarket, both of which are right there in walking distance from the statue.

Address: Allum Rd or County Rd, Kensington Ext 3/Oospoort (Eastgate in Afrikaans. Confusingly, there's an Eastgate in Sandton as well).
Coordinates: 26°10'53.29"S
28° 6'45.88"E

Gold Reef City — Right next door to the Apartheid Museum, this is a Victorian-era theme park with rides, a casino, and a genuine gold mine. You can watch the process of casting a bar of real gold. I believe you can still go down into the mine, which was opened in 1887. The centre of the theme park consists of genuine Victorian-era mining houses, with a bit of an American Wild West feel.

The entrance fee to the theme park is quite steep and doesn't cover all the tours, only the rides. There's easily enough entertainment there for a few days, especially for the kids.

Phone: +27 11 248-6800 and
+27 11 248 6896
Address: Follow Alamein/Northern Parkway Road and Gold Reef Road, Ormonde
Web: www.goldreefcity.co.za
Coordinates: 26°14'14.87"S
28° 0'53.16"E

The Hector Pieterson memorial —

This is close to Mandela's house. Hector Pieterson was one of the children killed by the Apartheid security forces in the Soweto uprising. He is famous because of a particular photograph of other children carrying away his body, fleeing the security forces.

Address: Cnr Phela and Khumalo Streets.
Coordinates: 26°14'7.18"S
27°54'29.14"E

The Houghton area — Old suburbs formerly inhabited by only the extremely wealthy mining magnates. Houghton is home to Nelson Mandela, when he is in Johannesburg. Many magnificent old houses can be seen in these suburbs, and the best view over these suburbs can be had from The Munro Drive.

Address: Cnr The Munro Drive/Elm Street, just off Houghton Drive
Coordinates: 26°10'19.48"S
28° 3'32.26"E

James Hall Museum of Transport — A large museum which features ancient cars, trains, and other forms of land transport. At Wemmer Pan.

Phone: +27 11 435 9718, 435-9485/6/7
Address: Pioneers' Park, Rosettenville Road, La Rochelle
Website: www.jhmt.org.za
Coordinates: 26°13'11.98"S 28° 3'1.33"E (Approximate, look out for brown signs)

Free entrance.

An old fire engine at the James Hall Museum of Transport

Johannesburg CBD — The Central Business District features dozens of impressive skyscrapers, as well as the venerable Art Gallery and Public Library.

Johannesburg's old central business district fell into ruin once Apartheid was dissolved, as most businesses evacuated the city centre and moved to Sandton to escape the rush of immigrants who were no longer prohibited from staying in the city by Apartheid laws. The city centre is slowly being refurbished and businesses are slowly moving back. One or two of the major banks kept their buildings and didn't move, but many of the other buildings have fallen into disrepair.

A moving experience, because it shows the former glory of the city (at the expense of others) and the sad levels of poverty that Apartheid created, giving you an insight into the reality of modern South Africa.

There are many interesting and cheap shops in the city centre, and there is a stunning view from the top of the Carlton Centre, the tallest building in Africa at 50 floors (223 m).

If you go to the city centre, don't forget to go to the museums at Newtown and Wits University, as they are nearby.

The Carlton Centre:
Phone: 011 441 4000
Address: 152 Commissioner Street, Johannesburg
Coordinates: 26°12'20.07"S 28° 2'48.31"E

There is parking in the basement, but it's quite hard to spot the entrance so you may have to drive around the building a few times.

There's also the old public library and the Johannesburg Art Gallery nearby (corner Edith Cavell and Wolmarans Street, Coordinates: 26°11'46.82"S, 28° 2'50.32"E).

Kliptown — Features Freedom Square, the Walter Sisulu Square of Dedication, where the freedom charter was signed in 1955; South Africa's original Bill of Rights.

Address: Union Road, Kliptown, Soweto
Web: www.waltersisulusquare.co.za
Coordinates: 26°16'42.34"S 27°53'21.46"E

Mandela Family Museum/ Mandela's House — Situated in Soweto, this is the former home of the first black president of South Africa, the freedom fighter and much-beloved patriarch of our country, Nelson Mandela.

Phone: +27 11 936 7754
Address: 8115, Orlando West, Soweto, cnr Vilakazi and Ngakane Streets
Web: www.mandelahouse.co.za
Coordinates: 26°14'18.70"S, 27°54'31.30"E

Melville — A quaint suburb at the foot of the SABC TV tower. Melville was built in the Victorian era and still has many original houses and churches standing, and an excellent selection of restaurants and night spots. Be aware that it is a hotspot for car theft, so park in front of an open restaurant if possible.

The majority of restaurants are in 7th street (closer to the CBD) or University Road (a few blocks further west). More on the restaurants featured in Melville will be discussed in the chapter on restaurants and shopping.

Coordinates: 26°10'37.99"S, 28° 0'30.59"E.

The Military History Museum — A fantastic collection of war memorabilia, old uniforms, weapons, medals, and vehicles from the various wars that South Africa has been involved in, including the Boer Wars, and the First and Second World Wars. There are also some machines from the Apartheid era.

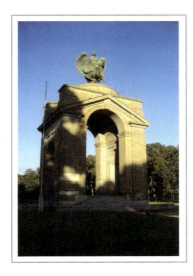

Probably the most exciting section is the vehicles section, which has a Dassault-Mirage Fighter Jet, a Messerschmitt jet, and a massive locally-made G6 howitzer from the Apartheid years when South Africa was invading other African states. There is also a mini submarine (one-man).

Phone: +27 (0) 11 646 5513
Address: Erlswold Way, Saxonwold
Web: www.militarymuseum.co.za
Coordinates: 26° 9'50.39"S
26° 9'50.39"S

A humorous snippet: a few years back, the government conducted a raid on the museum because they had been tipped off that the museum had stockpiled weapons!

Nelson Mandela Square — A piazza surrounded by high-class restaurants, featuring a large statue of Nelson Mandela. Details about the restaurants and shops will appear in a subsequent chapter.

Phone: +27 11 217 6000
Address: Cnr 5th Street and Rivonia Rd, Sandton
Website: www.nelsonmandelasquare.co.za
Coordinates: 26° 6'27.03"S, 28° 3'16.34"E

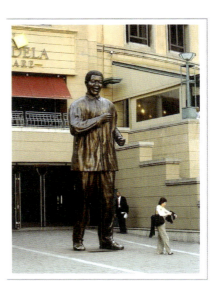

New Town and MuseumAfrica — Formerly a Victorian train station in the heart of Downtown Johannesburg, MuseumAfrica boasts an enormous collection of artifacts, ancient and modern.

Phone: +27 11 833 5624
Address: 121 Bree Street, Johannesburg
Websites:
www.newtown.co.za
www.joburg.org.za/content/view/252/51/
www.joburgnews.co.za/arts/arts_heritage.stm
Coordinates: 26°12'6.75"S 28° 1'51.07"E

There is also the nearby Market Theatre, and a number of interesting restaurants, as well as the SciBono museum (science, aimed at children) and some clubs. The details of these places will be given under later chapters.

Oppenheimer Tower and Credo Mutwa Cultural Village —Erected in honour of Ernest Oppenheimer, the mining magnate, the tower was built by workers who removed shacks and replaced them with proper houses that he organised the funding for.
    Credo Mutwa Cultural Village was built to depict African culture and folklore.

Phone: +27 11 938 1820
Address: Mphuti/Moahloli/Danny Kekana Street, Jabavu, Soweto
Coordinates: 26°14'37.01"S, 27°52'8.10"E

St. John's College — One of the original schools commissioned by Lord Milner in the late 1890s for British pupils, this school boasts a magnificent cathedral-like stone hall, and a chapel carved into the side of a cliff. Its architect was the renowned Sir Herbert Baker. Other similar schools designed by Sir Herbert or his students include Jeppe Boys' High School (in Kensington, shown below), King Edward VII (in Yeoville), and St. Stithians. St. John's is prettier than King Edward's, as more of the buildings are old. Jeppe only has two old buildings; the main building and hall, and the war memorial. The sun shines on this memorial's cenotaph on 11 November.

Contact Details:

St John's:
Phone: +27 11 645 3000
Address: St David Road, Houghton
Web: www.stjohnscollege.co.za
Coordinates: 26°10'35.62"S 28° 3'26.34"E

Jeppe Boys:
Phone: +27 11 614 1938
Address: Corner Good Hope & Roberts Avenue, Kensington
Web: www.jeppeboys.co.za
Coordinates: 26°12'2.33"S 28° 4'56.73"E

Bear in mind that these are functioning schools, not tourist attractions, so it may take a bit of legwork to persuade the security guards at the schools to let you in to take a look.

The Scots Highlanders monument on the nearby hill in Highland Road, Kensington, offers a magnificent panorama of the city. Be careful though, that there are no loiterers hanging around on the hill, before you go up. The hill's coordinates are: 26°12'1.24"S, 28° 5'5.74"E

Sophiatown — This suburb was demolished ruthlessly in 1955 by the Apartheid government, and re-settled with whites. They razed the homes of the defenceless former residents with graders and then renamed it Triomf ("Triumph")! Only the church was left standing. Sophiatown lies next door to Westdene and Melville. It has since been re-named back to Sophiatown ("Sophia" rhymes with "flyer").

I am not aware of any particular tourist attraction within Sophiatown; it was more of a cultural centre and a symbol of what the Apartheid government was about, and is remembered as such. Much of South African music originated there until 1955.

Address: Sophiatown, Johannesburg
Coordinates: 26°10'29.60"S
27°58'51.20"E

Soweto — The oldest township in South Africa, it was established to house a black labour force for the gold mines. The name is an acronym for "South West Township." It was the scene of the 1976 riots that ultimately led to the fall of Apartheid.

There are many places of significance in Soweto for those who are interested in the history of the struggle against Apartheid. I have listed the Mandela Family Museum, The Hector

Pieterson Memorial, The Cooling Towers, and Freedom Square.

Soweto is enormous — it is about 15 km top-to-bottom and the same across. I strongly recommend that you enter with a tour guide, or go with a packaged tour, or at the very least, a GPS, as you are very likely to get lost there.

Sunnyside Park Hotel — Probably the oldest hotel in Johannesburg, dating to back to 1895. A dark wood-panelled pub and a restaurant, inside a Victorian building.

Phone: +27 (0) 11 640 0400
Address: Princess of Wales Terrace, Parktown
Web: www.thesunnyside.co. za
Coordinates: 26°10'47.02"S
28° 2'48.30"E

Further Afield

In this section, I will mention a few places outside of Johannesburg itself, but within easy driving distance, which have recent historical interest.

Freedom Park — Just up another the hill north west of the Voortrekker Monument lies Freedom Park, a memorial to the Liberation Struggle.

Phone: +27 21 488 5060
Address: Koch Street, Salvokop, Pretoria
Web: www.freedompark.co. za
Coordinates: 25°45'59.46"S
28°11'20.01"E

Jan Smuts Museum — Home to General Smuts for forty years, located in the south eastern outskirts of Pretoria. Beautifully preserved. Jan Smuts ruled South Africa under the British Crown in the early 20th Century. He is famous not only as a statesman, but also as a philosopher.

Phone: +27 (012) 667-1176
Address: Jan Smuts Ave, Irene, Pretoria or 23rd Street West
Coordinates: 25°53'20.69"S, 28°13'55.60"E

Lesedi Cultural Village — showcases various tribal cultural homes and artefacts. Also includes songs and dance performances, and African food.

Phone: +27 12 205 1394
Address: Go up Malibongwe Drive in Randburg, and keep going north-by-north west for about 23km after Witkoppen Road. Pass Lanseria Airport.
Web: www.lesedi-conference.co.za
Coordinates: 25°50'16.09"S 27°53'2.82"E (there are some incorrect markers on Google Earth).

Melrose House — Another of Jan Smuts' homes, situated in Pretoria. Famous as the place where the treaty of Vereeniging was signed which ended the Boer War. (Source: www.melrosehouse.co.za).

Phone: +27 12 322 2805 / 322 0420
Address: 275 Jacob Maré Street, Pretoria across from Burger's Park. Free parking

is available at 280 Scheiding Street, to the south of Melrose House.
Web: www.melrosehouse.co.za
Coordinates: 25°45'18.16"S 28°11'32.94"E

Paul Kruger House and Church — The former home of the leader of the Transvaal Republic, as it was known before the British won the Boer wars and the Union of South Africa was formed. Built in 1884, it has been well-preserved.

The South African Republic, Traansvaal Republic or Boer Republic as it was variously known, gave its Dutch initials to South Africa: ZA (Zuid Afrika).

Phone: +27 12 326 9172
Address: 60 Church Street, Pretoria
GPS: 25°44'48.06"S 28°10'53.48"E

Sharpeville —The scene of the first major atrocity by the hands of the Apartheid security forces. There is a garden of remembrance opposite the police station, which commemorates the protesters — 69 of whom were killed and 180 injured, on March 21, 1960. The protest was about the 'dompas' system. Sharpeville is 45 km south of Soweto.

Address: Seeiso Street, Sharpeville

Coordinates: 26°40'37.62"S 27°53'30.47"E (approximate).

Union Buildings, Pretoria — The seat of South Africa's government in Pretoria (Parliament is in Cape Town).

A magnificent neoclassical building, and a national monument. The President of South Africa has his office here. Our equivalent of Capitol Hill or the White House.

Phone: +27 12 300 5200
Address: Government Avenue, Pretoria
Web: www.thepresidency.gov.za
Coordinates: 25°44'29.45"S 28°12'39.29"E

The Voortrekker Monument, Pretoria — An enormous structure erected in the Apartheid years to immortalise the Voortrekkers or Trekboers — the Dutch who fled the British into the South African hinterland. It is imposing and grandiose, and worth a visit. It has an impressive view from the top. On December 16, the sun shines directly down onto the cenotaph. See the information chapter under the 'holidays' section for the reason for this.

Phone: +27 12 326 6770
Address: Eeufees Road, Groenkloof, Pretoria
Web: www.voortrekkermon.org.za
Coordinates: 25°46'31.12"S 28°10'33.15"E

More information

For more information on Jo'burg's recent and distant past, including township tours, see:

www.pastexperiences.co.za
www.cultureclub.co.za

Chapter 6
Archaeological and Scientific Attractions

Introduction

There is much to see of archaeological and scientific interest in Johannesburg. Most of it is under the aegis of the University of the Witwatersrand, located just outside the old Johannesburg CBD, in a part of town called Braamfontein.

Johannesburg, or, more correctly speaking, the Sterkfontein area just out to the west of Johannesburg, is called the "Cradle of Humankind". This is because some of the oldest fossils of our most distant ancestors have been found there. Only Ethiopia has older fossils.

The University of the Witwatersrand, which runs Sterkfontein and hosts the Origins Museum, also has a strong Astronomy department, which has made substantial contributions to the science of galaxies. Furthermore, Wits also is home to Johannesburg's planetarium.

In Johannesburg Itself

MuseumAfrica, Newtown — Contains some anthropological displays. Formerly a Victorian train station. MuseumAfrica boasts an enormous collection of artifacts, ancient and modern.

Phone: +27 11 833 5624
Address: 121 Bree Street, Johannesburg
Web: www.joburg.org.za/content/view/252/51/
Coordinates: 26°12'6.75"S, 28° 1'51.07"E

The Observatory — Not originally intended as a tourist destination, you may be able to gain access to it by speaking to people at the Planetarium, University of the Witwatersrand, or by contacting SAASTA.

Phone: +27 12 392-9300
Address: Cnr Clerke and Innes Street, Observatory
Web: www.saasta.ac.za
Coordinates: 26°11'2.52"S, 28° 4'28.53"E.

The Origins Centre, University of the Witwatersrand — This museum showcases Bushman (!Xam/San) culture, and some relics of palaeontological finds made by Wits University in South Africa.

Recently, it has been altered to include some dinosaur automata and some dinosaur fossils found in the Karoo desert area of the Cape.

It also has many examples of ancient human fossils (though some are casts, as these fossils are too valuable to put on display).

You can even apply to get your DNA tested to see where your ancestors came from.

Phone: +27 11 717 4700
Address: Yale Road, Wits University, Braamfontein, Johannesburg
Web: www.origins.org.za
Coordinates: 26°11'31.81"S
28° 1'42.38"E

The Planetarium, University of the Witwatersrand — The Planetarium features a variety of shows, and explains the latest discoveries from NASA and other space agencies. The sky projector and dome is one of the oldest still in use. For city dwellers who have never seen the true night sky, it is a breathtaking experience. All the latest research is presented here regularly.

Phone: +27 11 717 1392
Address: Yale Road, Wits University, Braamfontein, Johannesburg
Web: www.planetarium.co.za
Coordinates: 26°11'19.10"S
28° 1'42.03"E

Scibono Centre, Newtown — An interactive museum on a variety of scientific topics aimed at the younger tourist. They have a Dassault-Mirage fighter jet suspended from the ceiling.

Phone: +27 11 639 8400
Address: Cnr Miriam Makeba and President Street, Newtown
Websites: www.sci-bono.co.za
www.newtown.co.za
Coordinates: 26°12'13.16"S
28° 1'57.80"E

Further Afield

Transvaal Museum (Natural History Museum), Pretoria — Enormous, and well worth the forty minute drive from Johannesburg, it covers everything from animals ancient and modern, to geology. It was founded in 1892. Its nearest rival in South Africa is the Natural History Museum in Cape Town. I believe that the actual skull of Mrs Ples, one of the finds from Sterkfontein, resides here. It lies opposite the Pretoria City Hall.

Phone: +27 12 322 7632
Address: 1 Paul Kruger Street, Pretoria
Web: www.nfi.org.za/tmpage.html
Coordinates: 25°45'11.09"S, 28°11'19.54"E

Sterkfontein Caves and Maropeng — You can tour an ancient cave system inhabited millions of years ago by our distant ancestors.

Recently (April 2010) an exciting new find was made in this area (*Australopithecus sediba*), dating back to about 1.95 million years ago, of almost-complete skeletons, which were put on display at the Origins Centre at Wits.

There is also an impressive new museum (Maropeng).

If you have to choose one tourist attraction to go to in Johannesburg, make it the Apartheid Museum. If you can do two, then your second choice should be Sterkfontein Caves and Maropeng.

Maropeng
Phone: +27 14 577 9000
Address: 6.2km after Sterkfontein caves turnoff on Route R 563, Sterkfontein
Web: www.maropeng.co.za
Coordinates: 25°58'12.86"S 27°39'46.89"E

Vertebra at Sterkfontein Caves

Sterkfontein Caves
Phone: +27 14 577 9000
Address: Sterkfontein Caves Road, 2.3km
after N14 turnoff on Route R 563,
Sterkfontein
Web: www.maropeng.co.za
Coordinates: 26° 1'6.56"S, 27°43'57.42"E
Map

www.maropeng.co.za/images/uploads/
larger_map.jpg

Wonder Cave — They have beautiful
stalagmites and stalactites at this cave.
Near Sterkfontein, located within the
Rhino and Lion Nature Reserve, my
most recommended game park.

Phone: +27 11 957 0106
Address: Wondercave Rd., Kromdraai.
Follow the Kromdraai road, turn left into
Main road. Follow that east for about
4km.
Web: http://www.primeorigins.co.za/
sterkfontein_whs/attractions/
www.rhinolion.co.za
Coordinates: 25°58'11.53"S
27°46'16.41"E

More information

For more information on Jo'burg's
recent and distant past, including
township tours, see:

www.pastexperiences.co.za
www.cultureclub.co.za

44

Chapter 7
Shopping

Introduction

There are many large shopping malls, and more restaurants than I could possibly list, in Johannesburg. It is truly Africa's shopping capital. This selection below consists only of my personal recommendations. There are also a large number of franchises in Johannesburg which you will start to recognise over time. Generally, franchises can be relied on for consistency.

In Johannesburg Itself

I recommend the following malls, as they are close to the airport and the future Gautrain routes. They are all large, multi-storey, with generous parking. These malls all contain large grocery stores, movie theatres, and many restaurants — both fast-food and formal, sit-down places. Two of the malls — Rosebank and Eastgate, have a flea market nearby. There are at least four other major malls, but they are somewhat far from tourist locations so I have not mentioned them.

Eastgate Shopping Centre — This mall is en-route to the city centre from the airport. It has a sister mall adjacent to it called **Park Meadows**, and there is also the nearby **Bedford Centre** mall (these three malls are all within a few blocks of each other).

Eastgate has the widest range of stores of all the malls I enumerate, and is one of the oldest in Johannesburg. It seems easy to get lost in it, but just remember that it is technically a square shape, so if you keep walking, you'll come back to where you started. It is one of the biggest malls in SA.

I recommend that you avoid watching movies here as the theatres are usually crowded. Watch out for the beggars at the traffic lights between Eastgate and Bruma on Marcia Road; they seem to think that washing car windows is a valuable service. To avoid them, drive over the bridge from Eastgate's upper parking level, to Bruma.

The main reason to choose Eastgate is if you want to go to Bruma as well, or if you want to see the statue of George Harrison (below).

45

Phone: +27 11 479 6000
Address: Nicol Rd, Bedfordview
Web: www.eastgatecentre.co.za
Coordinates: 26°10'52.39"S
28° 7'4.44"E

Greenstone Shopping Mall —
Greenstone is a very new mall, built in a straight line, with most things that you could want. The movie theatres here are usually deserted, so if you want to watch a mainstream Hollywood movie, this is the mall that I recommend.

Most easily accessed by taking the Modderfontein offramp from the N3/N12 North/Pretoria-bound motorway, and following the Edenvale signs eastwards. The second traffic light to your left is the mall entrance. Watch out for the vendors at this intersection, they like playing tricks on you to get you to buy their stuff, especially the "your tyre is flat" gag and the "it's for free" gag.

Phone: +27 11 524 0445
Address: Cnr. Modderfontein Rd and Van Riebeeck Avenue, Edenvale.
Web: www.greenstonemall.co.za
Coordinates: 26° 7'15.06"S
28° 8'26.24"E

The Mall of Rosebank

Half-way between the city centre and Sandton, near the zoo, is the popular Rosebank Mall. A more up-market mall, but rather old and small, with a somewhat limited selection of stores compared to Eastgate or Sandton. The primary reason to go to this mall is for their Art Nouveau cinema in the basement, or for the flea market, or for the nice selection of restaurants built around the parking lot. The Art Nouveau cinema features mainly European and art house or indie movies.

There is another mall across the parking lot from the old one, called The Zone. That mall has mainly teenagers' clothing stores and a cinema which shows Hollywood and Bollywood movies, plus there's a big music store.

Rosebank also has a flea market on Sunday in its upper-level parking areas, and regular African musicians and buskers.

Phone: +27 11 442 5822
Address: Enter at Cnr. Cradock and Baker Street, Rosebank.

Web: www.rosebank.co.za
Coordinates: 26° 8'49.81"S
28° 2'33.19"E

Cinema Franchises & DVDs

We have two cinema franchises here — *Ster Kinekor* and *NuMetro*. Please be aware that only Ster Kinekor and NuMetro are permitted to import DVDs into our country, so any DVDs which do not have their logos on the back cover are likely pirated, stolen, and funding terrorism. You wouldn't steal a car, now would you? Be aware that we use Zone-2 DVDs here, like the UK and Europe. There are also a number of movies that are worth buying about Jo'burg and South Africa, e.g. *Shaka Zulu, Catch a Fire, Goodbye Bafana, Stander, The Gods Must be Crazy, District 9, Tsotsi, Blood Diamond, Forgiveness, Invictus*, etc.

Sandton City

Sandton City is the oldest mall in Johannesburg. It contains pretty much every kind of store you may wish for. It also has a movie theatre section, but again, like Eastgate, it is usually crowded. The main advantage to Sandton is that there are some nice hotels and restaurants nearby, especially at Mandela Square. You can get to Mandela Square via a bridge from Sandton City.

Phone: +27 11 217 6000
Address: Cnr 5th Street and Rivonia Roads, Sandton
Web: www.sandton-city.co.za
Coordinates: 26° 6'31.69"S
28° 3'19.33"E

Nelson Mandela Square

Right next door to to Sandton City is **Nelson Mandela Square**, accessible via a shop-lined pedestrian bridge. It features an open piazza with fountains and exclusive restaurants. Also features the statue of N. R. Mandela.

Phone: +27 11 217 6000
Address: Cnr 5th Street and Rivonia Roads, Sandton
Web: www.nelsonmandelasquare.co.za
Coordinates: 26° 6'31.69"S
28° 3'19.33"E

Open Air Markets / Flea Markets

Boksburg Flea Market — Enormous. Close to an large, interesting plant nursery, where you can watch the jets landing at OR Tambo Airport.

Address: Rondebult Rd offramp, Left into Cynthia Rd (parallel to North Rand Rd), Boksburg. Look for the large green tin roof.
Coordinates: 26°10'42.58"S
28°14'17.00"E

Bruma Flea Market — Across the motorway from Eastgate. They sell primarily Chinese and other cheap goods. There is an entrance fee. I favour this flea market over the others.

Address: 49 Ernest Oppenheimer Drive
Coordinates: 26°10'41.25"S
28° 6'43.18"E

The Bryanston Organic Market — A slightly misleading name, as it's a flea market, primarily, that happens to have some organic food stalls, including gluten-free breads, organic cheeses and vegetables. They have a wide range of stalls.

Phone: +27 11 706 3671
Address: At Michael Mount Waldorf School, Culross Road (off Main Road), Bryanston.
Web: www.bryanstonorganicmarket.co.za
Coordinates: 26° 2'42.64"S, 28° 1'39.92"E

The Oriental Plaza — Mainly middle-eastern and Indian goods, such as fabrics, brasses and curries. Try the samoosas (curry-filled, triangular, deep-fried pastries). Note that the majority of stall-owners are Muslim and that therefore the stalls are shut on Friday at lunch time for prayers. The Oriental Plaza is also closed on Sunday. This is the best place to go for cheap clothing, fabric, and Indian spices. It is well worth a visit.

Phone: +27 11 836 4674
Address: Bree, Malherbe, Lilian, Main & Avenue, Streets, Fordsburg, Johannesburg
Web: www.orientalplaza-fordsburg.co.za
Coordinates: 26°12'12.92"S,
28° 1'24.73"E

Rosebank — Rosebank's flea market occurs on a Sunday in the parking lot of the mall, selling mainly Africana and artworks, as well as esoterica and spices. Very popular and very tourist-oriented. Address and contact details are as per Rosebank Mall.

Chapter 8
Restaurants

Dining

Johannesburg has a wide variety of fast-food places and restaurants, many of which are good quality, even if they are franchises. In fact, of all the cities I have been to, Johannesburg, in my opinion, outstrips them all, for the sheer number and quality of food places. You cannot be bored of food here.

I have not given the addresses or phone numbers of fast-food places because they are everywhere. I will only give exact details of a particular branch if I think they have excelled or if they happen to be hard to find. This chapter also contains a *short* list of the sit-down restaurants that I recommend. All of them are highly-rated.

Incidentally, South Africa produces its own beef and has never had a mad cow disease incident. Meat is relatively cheap here, and thus is served in large portions (you can typically get 500g/1Lb steaks at restaurants).

I have placed a star rating next to each place that I've been to (no stars means that I've not been to it). Three stars means "acceptable", fewer means "avoid". *Remember, these are only my opinions*. The stars here have nothing to do with an establishment's *actual* rating.

PS. Our American visitors: when calling for the bill at a restaurant, you ask for the *bill*, not the cheque.

Fast Food and Take-Away (take out)

Most of these places will let you sit and eat if you wish.

You can also call **Mr Delivery** on +27 11 507-2800 to order from whichever franchises are in your area, instead of trying to find them. Please tip your delivery man at least R 10. Their branches are listed on their website: *https://www.mrdelivery.com/mrdelivery.php*. Each company's website lists its stores or branches.

Burgers and Fries, Roadhouse Food

Bimbo's ⊚⊚ — Nice schwarmas though. They run 24/7. I suggest the Beyers Naudé Drive (Northcliff/Risidale) branch. Coordinates: 26° 8'22.65"S, 27°58'43.44"E. www.bimbos.co.za

Black Steer ⊚⊚⊚⊚ — Great burgers. Rosebank Mall (Bulldog's Pub). They're due to be bought out by Steers, however, so they may re-brand or close down completely.

MacDonald's ⊙⊙ — mcdonalds.co.za

Steers ⊙⊙⊙⊙ — Ubiquitous and good. Vegetarian available. www.steers.co.za.

Wimpy ⊙⊙⊙ — Actually an eat-in place but a very common franchise. Breakfasts aren't bad, burgers oily. Their club sandwiches are good. Don't bother with their steaks. www.wimpy.co.za

Oriental, Stir-Fry and Sushi

Kauai ⊙⊙⊙⊙ — www.kauai.co.za
Kung-Fu Kitchen ⊙⊙⊙ — www.kungfukitchen.co.za
Teriyaki Experience ⊙⊙⊙⊙⊙ — www.teriyakiexperience.com
Yo Sushi ⊙⊙⊙⊙ — 3rd Ave, corner 2nd 7th Street, Parktown North. Coordinates: 26° 8'42.88"S, 28° 1'43.49"E. There may be a branch in Sandton.

Middle-Eastern

Anat ⊙⊙⊙⊙⊙ — Eastgate, Sandton City, and Rosebank Mall. www.anat.co.za
Mi Vami ⊙⊙⊙⊙ — Corlett Drive, Birnam, opposite the entrance to Melrose Arch. Coordinates: 26° 7'47.13"S, 28° 4'5.47"E. Also one in Linksfield opposite King David School, Club Street, Coordinates: 26° 9'46.49"S, 28° 6'26.21"E. www.mivami.co.za

Chicken

Al's Gourmet Chicken ⊙⊙⊙⊙ — Corlett Drive, Birnam, opposite the entrance to Melrose Arch. Coordinates: 26° 7'47.13"S, 28° 4'5.47"E.

Fontana Roastery ⊙⊙⊙ — www.fontanachicken.co.za

KFC ⊙⊙⊙ — Their chips are usually terrible, but the rest is good. www.kfc.co.za

Nando's ⊙⊙⊙⊙ — Spicy, Portuguese. www.nandos.co.za

Chicken Licken — www.chickenlicken.co.za

Pizza

Most pizza places use pre-made bases and/or electric ovens (except Pizza Perfect and Mimmo's, but Mimmo's is more of a sit-down restaurant).

Debonair's ⊙⊙ — www.debonairs.co.za

Pizza Perfect ⊙⊙⊙⊙ — Wood fired, freshly-made thin bases. They also do chicken. www.pizzaperfect.co.za
Roman's — www.romanspizza.co.za
St. Elmo's ⊙⊙⊙ — Wood fired but the bases don't seem freshly-made. www.stelmos.co.za
Scooter's ⊙⊙ — www.scooterspizza.co.za

Fish and Chips

Fish and Chips — www.fishandchips.co.za. They serve proper onion rings, deep fried sausages and 'slaptjips' too.
Fishaways — www.fishaways.co.za
Ocean Basket — Actually an eat-in place, they do take-aways. www.oceanbasket.co.za

Indian

Shahi Edenvale ⊙⊙ — Van Riebeeck Avenue, between Hendrik Potigieter and 4th Street. Coordinates: 26° 8'31.12"S, 28° 9'12.74"E. I can't think of any other Indian take-away places. There is a better *Shahi* in Norwood.

Café-style places, light lunches

Some of these act as bars or pubs at night, especially *News Café* and *Q.Ba*.

Café Nescafé ⊙⊙⊙⊙ — www.cafenescafe.co.za. There's one at Melrose Arch.

Capello ⊙⊙⊙⊙ — they do dinners as well. Grant Avenue, Norwood, and right next door to the Greenside Doppio Zero. www.cappello.co.za

Doppio Zero ⊙⊙⊙⊙⊙ — the one at Greenside is the best. Cnr Gleneagles & Barry Hertzog. Coordinates: 26° 8'47.72"S, 28° 0'31.45"E. They are very popular so you should make a table booking. www.doppio.co.za

Espresso Caffe & Bistro — Phone: +27 11 447 8700. Address: 23A 4th Avenue, Parkhurst. Coordinates: 26° 8'24.68"S, 28° 1'2.25"E.

Europa/Fego ☺☺☺☺ — www.antimo.co.za. There's one at Rosebank Mall and Melrose Arch.

Fournos Bakery ☺☺☺☺☺ — www.fournos.co.za. See below on bakeries.

JB's Corner — Address: 3 The High St, Melrose Arch, Melrose. Phone: +27 11 684 2999. Coordinates: 26° 1'28.27"S, 28° 0'45.61"E. www.jbscorner.co.za

M&A ☺☺☺☺ — I believe it stands for Maestro and Antonio. That may help in a Google Search. There's one at the Rosebank Mall.

Moemas — A *patisserie*. Phone: +27 11 788 7725. Address: Parktown Quarter (opposite the parking lot), Parktown North. Web: www.moemas.co.za. Coordinates: 26° 8' 41.79" S, 28° 1' 44.24" E

Mugg & Bean ☺☺☺☺ — www.themugg.com. Everywhere.

News Café ☺☺☺☺ — Rivonia Boulevard, Rivonia, or Sandton CBD (Fredman Drive), or Campus Square, Kingsway Avenue, Auckland Park, Coordinates 26°10'55.81"S, 28° 0'11.06"E. www.newscafe.co.za.

Nice — Breakfast and lunch, Tuesday to Sunday. Phone: +27 11 788 6286. Address: Cnr Fourth Avenue and 14th Street, Parkhurst. Coordinates: 26° 8'25.25"S, 28° 1'2.42"E (approximate).

Nino's ☺☺☺☺☺ — the one at Rosebank Mall is best. See the chapter on Shopping. www.ninos.co.za

Primi Piatti ☺☺☺☺ — primipiatti.primi-network.co.za. There's one at Rosebank, The Zone.

Q.Ba ☺☺☺☺ — www.qbacaffe.co.za

Service Station ☺☺☺☺☺ — You choose your food from a buffet and weigh it to get the price. Interesting shop attached. Phone: +27 11 726 1701. Address: Ninth Avenue and Rustenburg Road, Melville. Web: www.bamboo-online.co.za. Coordinates: 26°10'28.01"S, 28° 0'48.92"E

Catz Pyjamas — functions as a nightclub at night. Phone: +27 11 726 8596. Address: 12 Main Rd (University Drive), Melville. Web: www.catzpyjamas.co.za. Coordinates: 26°10'37.86"S, 28° 0'4.13"E

Pubs and Cocktail Lounges

See the chapter on Nightlife.

Bakeries

Most grocery stores have in-store bakeries, so you shouldn't struggle to find fresh bread. There are, however, a few bakeries worth mentioning:

Doppio Zero, *Greenside*. See above under cafés and light lunches. They have a bakery.

Fournos ☺☺☺☺☺ — Fournos is the best bakery and makes the best croissants in Johannesburg. www.fournos.co.za

Dunkeld branch:
Phone: +27 11 325 2110/1
Address: Dunkeld West Centre, Cnr. Jan Smuts & Bompas
Dunkeld, Johannesburg
Web: www.fournos.co.za
Coordinates: 26° 7'53.59"S
28° 2'6.89"E

Rosebank branch:
Address: Enter at Cnr. Cradock and Baker Street, Rosebank.
Web: www.rosebank.co.za
Coordinates: 26° 8'49.81"S
28° 2'33.19"E

Koljander — A "tuisnywerheid" or "home industry" place in Melville, Main Rd/University Drive. They make all kinds of authentic South African confections, including *koeksisters* and *melktert*. Winner of *Best of Joburg* award.

Phone: +27 11 726-6282/3/4
Address: 11 Main Road, Melville
Web: www.koljander.co.za
Coordinates: 26°10'39.04"S
28° 0'4.08"E (approximate)

Formal Eat-in Restaurants

There are thousands of eat-in restaurants in Johannesburg, and I couldn't hope to list them all even if I tried. The below list consists merely of my recommendations. For a better idea of what is available, try some restaurant-finder websites, such as www.dining-out.co.za, www.eatout.co.za, and www.what2night.co.za.

Smoking

All restaurants and malls should be assumed to be non-smoking venues. Some restaurants have closed-off smoking sections or outdoor sections. If you smoke, that's where you should go. If you have children, please consider refraining from smoking for an hour or two; the smoking sections in SA restaurants are closed-off and very smoggy and you are ruining your children's health.

African

Abyssinia — Ethiopian/Eritrean. Very authentic, including Injera bread and coffee ritual. Owner walked here from Ethiopia, which is about 3900km to the north. Recommended, but not "high class". Very cheap. There used to be a few other Ethiopian places but they have gone out of business.

Phone: 072 918 8824
Address: Cnr. Queen Street and Robert's Avenue, Kensington.
Coordinates: 26°11'21.21"S 28° 6'28.95"E

Afrodisiac ☺☺☺ — Attached to a plant nursery, acts as a nightclub at night. Also has a small petting zoo.

Phone: +27 11 443 9990
Address: Corner Club Street, Civin & Linksfield Drive, Linksfield
Web: www.theafrodisiac.co.za
Coordinates: 26° 8'54.92"S, 28° 7'32.14"E

Cool Runnings ☺☺☺☺ — Jamaican food; try Bob's Burning Spear. They also have an extensive cocktail menu. They act as a bar at night and sometimes have shows in the "dungeon". A must-see.

Phone: +27 11 482 4786
Address: 27 4th Avenue, Melville
Web: www.coolrunnings.co.za
Coordinates: 26°10'35.35"S, 28° 0'4.83"E

Gramadoelas — Exotic game such as crocodile and traditional African food, even mopani worms (caterpillars).

Phone: +27 11 838 6960
Address: Market Theatre, Bree Street, Newtown
Web: www.gramadoelas.co.za
Coordinates: 26°12'6.75"S 28° 1'51.07"E

Lekgotla

Phone: +27 11 884 9555
Address: 5th Street, Nelson Mandela Square, Sandton

Coordinates: 26° 6'26.81"S 28° 3'15.76"E

Mamma's Shebeen ☺☺☺☺☺, aka Mama Tembo's. — Serves township fare. Located in Greenside. It's advisable to book. Very themed and authentic-looking. A must-see.

Phone: +27 82 965 2640, +27 84 652 7851, +27 78 804 6804 (mobiles)
Address: 18 Gleneagles Road, Greenside
Web: www.mammas.co.za
Coordinates: 26° 8'46.25"S, 28° 0'36.42"E

Moyo ☺☺☺☺☺ — Primarily north-African food. A franchise. I recommend the one at Zoo Lake, as it gives you an excuse to go to the lake, the Zoo and the War Museum on the same day.
      If you go to the Spier Wine Estate in Cape Town, they have a buffet. A Must-see. Very pricy. The Melrose Arch branch has a cute rock feature inside.
Web: www.moyo.co.za

Zoo Lake Branch:
Phone: +27 11 646 0058
Address: 1 Prince of Wales Drive, Parkview
Coordinates: 26° 9'26.63"S, 28° 1'46.18"E

Melrose Arch Branch:
Phone: +27 11 684 1477
Address: Melrose Square, High Street, Melrose Arch, Athol Oaklands Road
Coordinates: 26° 8'2.18"S, 28° 4'5.24"E. (Google Earth has incorrect coordinates. These are correct.)

Wandie's Place — Probably the most popular restaurant in Soweto, featuring real South African township fare. A must-see for any tourist to Johannesburg. Be warned, it is heavily booked out, so you should arrange to go with a tour group.

Phone: +27 11 982 2796
Address: 618 Makhalamele Street, Dube, Soweto, less than 2km from Hector Pieterson and Mandela's House
Web: http://www.joburg.org.za/content/view/988/159/
Coordinates: 26°14'15.68"S 27°53'23.10"E (approximate)

Fish

Cape Town Fish Market

Phone: +27 +11 884 8529
Address: Shop 21, Banking Level, Sandton City, Cnr Rivonia & 5th Street, Sandton
Web: www.ctfm.com
Coordinates: 26° 6'31.69"S 28° 3'19.33"E

Montego Bay ☺☺☺☺☺ — A fish restaurant. Good sushi. A bit pricy.

Phone: +27 11 883 6407
Address: 5th Street, Nelson Mandela Square, Sandton
Web: www.montegobay.co.za
Coordinates: 26° 6'26.81"S 28° 3'15.76"E

French

Coachman's Inn ☺☺☺☺ — A very long-standing restaurant, set in a quaint 1700s-style interior.

Phone: +27 11 706 7269
Address: 29 Peter Place, Lyme Park, Bryanston, Sandton
Coordinates: 26° 4'52.55"S 28° 1'3.11"E

Le Canard — A long-standing restaurant, very highly rated.
Phone: +27 11 884 4597
Address: 163 Rivonia Rd, Morningside, Sandton
Web: www.lecanard.co.za
Coordinates: 26°5'47.21"S 28°3'22.96"E

Fusion

The Bell Pepper

Phone: +27 11 615 7531
Address: 176 Queen Street, Kensington
Coordinates: 26°11'9.70"S
28° 6'23.59"E

Café MezzaLuna ☺☺☺☺☺ — A la carte, a bit of a hangout for artists.

Phone: +27 11 482 2477
Seventh Street, Melville
Coordinates: 26°10'34.51"S
28°0'31.58"E

Cilantro — Lunch and dinner, Tuesday to Sunday. They describe their food as "Meditterasian"

Phone: +27 11 327 4558
Address: 24 Fourth Avenue, Parkhurst
Coordinates: 26° 8'25.25"S
28° 1'2.42"E (approximate)

George's on Fourth

Phone: +27 11 447 7705
Address: 21 Fourth Avenue, Parkhurst
Coordinates: 26° 8'25.25"S
28° 1'2.42"E (approximate)

Soulsa

Phone: +27 11 482 5572
Address: 16 7th St., Melville
Web: soulsa.wordpress.com
Coordinates: 26°10'30.60"S
28° 0'32.51"E (Google Earth has incorrect coordinates).

Indian

Bombay Blues

Phone: +27 11 447 3210

Address: Shop 6, Standard Bank building, Cnr Cradock and Tyrwhitt Avenues, Rosebank
Web: www.bombayblues.co.za
Coordinates: 26° 8'41.95"S
28° 2'32.03"E

Cumin and Coriander

Phone: +27 11 616 7734
Address: 153 Queen Street, Kensington
Coordinates: 26°11'15.81"S
28° 6'26.86"E

Karma ☺☺☺☺

Phone: +27 11 646 8555
Address: Corner Greenfields and Gleneagles Road, Greenside
Coordinates: 26° 8'47.99"S
28° 0'44.98"E

Saffron

Phone: +27 11 883 5288
Address: Grayston Shopping Centre, Strathavon, Sandton
Coordinates: 26° 5'59.97"S
28° 3'58.61"E

Sahib — Same franchise as Shahi.

Phone: +27 11 268 6669
Address: Shop No.6 Illovo Square, Rivonia Rd, Illovo

Coordinates: 26° 7'39.48"S
26° 7'39.48"S

Shahi Khana ⊚⊚⊚⊚ — Go on a Tuesday night, because they have an all-you-can-eat buffet for R 70. Booking is essential. Ice-cream and naan bread included. Be careful of the green sauce.

Phone: +27 11 728 8157
Address: 80 Grant Avenue, Norwood
Coordinates: 26° 9'29.39"S
26° 9'29.39"S

Italian

Café della Salute ⊚⊚⊚ — They sell 'spaghetti' ice cream, and they have build-your-own breakfast option.

Phone: +27 11 784 2145
Address: 5th Street, Nelson Mandela Square, Sandton
Coordinates: 26° 6'26.81"S
28° 3'15.76"E

Ciao Baby Cucina ⊚⊚⊚⊚⊚ — A franchise. Excellent food. Professional service. More upmarket than Mimmo's.
Website: ciaobabycucina.co.za

The Eastgate Branch: (the original)
Phone: +27 11 616 5102/4999
Address: 43 Bradford Road Corner Nicol and Bradford Rd, Bedforview

Coordinates: 26°10'52.39"S, 28° 7'4.44"E

The Monte Casino Branch:
Phone: +27 11 511 0212/3
Address: Montecasino Piazza, Montecasino Boulevard, Fourways
Coordinates: 26° 1'28.27"S, 28° 0'45.61"E

Mimmo's ⊚⊚⊚⊚ — Good steaks, wood-fired pizza, very reasonably priced. Rated the best Italian franchise two years in a row.

Phone: +27 11 392 4522
Address: Enter at Cnr. Cradock and Baker Street, Rosebank.
Web: www.mimmos.co.za
Coordinates: 26° 8'49.81"S
28° 2'33.19"E.

Tortellino D'Oro ⊚⊚⊚⊚⊚ — Excellent.

Phone: +27 11 483 1249
Address: Cnr Pretoria & Kruger Streets, Oaklands Shopping Centre, Oaklands
Web: www.tortellino.co.za
Coordinates: 26° 8'47.64"S
28° 3'48.79"E

Mexican

Cantina Tequila ⊚⊚⊚⊚ — Latin dance available.

Phone: +27 795 2132

Address: Shop 8A, 1st Floor, Banbury Crossing, Cnr Malibongwe (Hans Strijdom) & Olievenhout, North Riding
Web: www.cantinatequila.co.za (Cape Town only, but it will give you an idea)
Coordinates: 26° 3'42.96"S 27°57'18.18"E

Also 4th Avenue, Linden.
Phone: +27 82 448 9789.

Middle Eastern and Greek

Beirut ☺☺☺☺ — Lebanese food, with some specialities. Book in advance.
Parkmore Branch:
Phone: +27 11 884 1015
Address: 136A, 11th Street in Parkmore, Sandton
Coordinates: 26° 5'58.53"S, 28° 2'50.94"E

Bedfordview Branch:
They require smart casual clothes, and have belly dancers.
Phone: +27 11 450 2392
Address: Shop 2, The Kloof Shopping Complex, Corner of Kloof & Arterial (N12), Bedfordview
Coordinates: 26°11'4.89"S, 28° 8'4.60"E

Pappa's ☺☺☺☺☺ — Greek food and meze. A bit pricy, but they have a belly dancer on Fridays and Saturdays and you can break plates that you can purchase specifically for this purpose. Advisable to book.

Phone: +27 11 884 9991
Address: 5th Street, Nelson Mandela Square, Sandton
Web: www.pappasrestaurant.co.za
Coordinates: 26° 6'26.81"S, 28° 3'15.76"E

Plaka — Greek cuisine.

Phone: +27 11 268 6969
Address: Shop G4 Illovo Thrupps Centre, 204 Oxford Road, Illovo
Web: www.plaka.co.za
Coordinates: 26° 7'48.61"S 28° 2'58.22"E

Schwarma Co. ☺☺☺☺☺ — Middle-eastern. The rib portions are enormous. You should book in advance.

Phone: +27 11 483 1776
Address: 71 Grant Avenue, Norwood.
Web: www.schwarmacompany.co.za
Coordinates: 26° 9'26.82"S 28° 4'34.95"E

Sheikh's Palace — Lebanese. Features belly dancers.

Phone: +27 11 807 4119
Address: Cnr Rivonia Rd & 9th Ave, Rivonia
Web: www.sheikhspalace.co.za
Coordinates: 26° 3'27.85"S 28° 3'37.16"E

Zahava's — Many different exotic cuisines including middle eastern, Jewish, Russian, etc. Lunch only.
Phone: +27 11 728 6511
Address: 47 Grant Avenue

Coordinates: 26° 9'35.98"S
28° 4'34.24"E (approximate)

Oriental, Stir-Fry and Sushi

Cranks — weird decor, including a large metal scorpion and Barbies in compromising positions. Thai and Vietnamese cuisine.

Phone: +27 11 880 3442
Address: Shop 169 Rosebank Mall, Cradock Avenue, Rosebank
Coordinates: 26° 8'49.81"S
28° 2'33.19"E

Imperial Palace

Phone: +27 11 883 0923
Address: 5th Street, Nelson Mandela Square, Sandton
Coordinates: 26° 6'26.81"S, 28° 3'15.76"E

Kai Thai ☺☺☺☺ — Thai food. They are a franchise with many fast-food outlets.

Montecasino Branch:
Phone: +27 11 511 1844
Address: Shop U61 Montecasino, Cnr William Nicol and Witkoppen Roads, Fourways
Web: www.kaithai.com

Coordinates: 26° 1'28.27"S
28° 0'45.61"E

Orient — A glamorous oriental restaurant. Rated five star. Pricy.
Phone: +27 11 684 1616
Address: 4 The High Street, Melrose Arch
Web: www.melrosearch.co.za
Coordinates: 26° 1'28.27"S
28° 0'45.61"E.

Rainbow Sushi ☺☺☺☺

Phone: +27 11 483 0293
Address: 74 Grant Ave, Norwood
Coordinates: 26° 9'29.39"S
26° 9'29.39"S (approximate).

Red Chamber ☺☺☺☺☺ — Hyde Park shopping Centre. Japanese and Chinese food. Excellent quality.

Phone: +27 11 325 6048
Address: Hyde Park Shopping Centre, Jan Smuts Avenue, Hyde Park
Coordinates: 26° 7'37.23"S, 28° 2'0.50"E

Ruby Grapefruit — Rated highly for sushi.

Phone: +27 11 880 3673
Address: 24 Fourth Avenue, Parkhurst
Coordinates: 26° 8'25.25"S, 28° 1'2.42"E (approximate)

Soi — Vietnamese.

Phone: +27 11 726-5775
Address: Cnr 7th Str & 3rd Ave, Melville
Coordinates:: 26°10'35.17"S,
28° 0'31.58"E

Tsunami ☺☺☺☺☺ — Japanese Teppanyaki. Good food and reasonably good service. They also serve steaks, good wines, and sushi.

Phone: +27 11 880 8409 / +27 11 442 9109
Address: Rosebank mall, upper level. Enter at Cnr. Cradock and Baker Street, Rosebank.
Web: www.tsunamisa.co.za
Coordinates: 26° 8'49.81"S 28° 2'33.19"E

They also have a branch in the mall on the corner of Outspan Rd and Rivonia Rd, Morningside. I prefer the Rosebank branch.

2 Thai 4 ☺☺☺☺☺ — a long-standing Thai restaurant.

Phone: +27 11 440 3000
Address: 59 Corlett Drive, Melrose
Web: www.2thai4.co.za
Coordinates: 26° 7'51.22"S 28° 3'51.87"E

Wangthai — Thai food.

Phone: +27 11 784 8484
Address: Shop 120, Upper Floor, 5th Street, Nelson Mandela Square, Sandton
Web: www.wangthai.co.za
Coordinates: 26° 6'26.81"S 28° 3'15.76"E

Yamato — Japanese.

Phone: +27 11 268 0511/12
Address: Illovo Thrupps Centre, 198 Oxford Road, Illovo
Web: www.yamato.co.za
Coordinates: 26° 7'48.61"S 28° 2'58.22"E

Yo Sushi ☺☺☺☺ — A franchise.

Parktown North Branch:
Address: 3rd Ave, corner 2nd 7th Street, Parktown North.

Coordinates: 26° 8'42.88"S, 28° 1'43.49"E

Sandton Branch:
Phone: +27 7836166
Address: Shop U49, Village Walk Ctr, Maude St, Sandown
Coordinates: 26° 6'13.13"S, 26° 6'13.13"S (Google Earth has the wrong coordinates for Village Walk).

Portuguese

Adega ☺☺☺☺ — A Portuguese franchise. The original branch is in Kensington.
Web: www.adegas.co.za

The Sandton Franchise Branch:
Phone: +27 11 883 0072/3
Address: Village Walk Shopping Centre, Cnr. Maude and Rivonia Roads.
Coordinates: 26° 6'13.13"S, 26° 6'13.13"S
(Google Earth has the wrong coordinates for Village Walk).

The Original Adega:
Address: Robert's Avenue, Kensington
Coordinates: 26°11'59.93"S 28° 4'44.34"E (approximate)

Canoa

Phone: +27 11 443 6258

Address: Linksfield Terrace Shopping Centre, Linksfield Road, just before the N12/N3 offramp.
Coordinates: 26° 8'54.61"S
28° 7'40.45"E

Nuno's and Xai Xai — right next door to each other, both offer Portuguese food. Xai Xai is more of a cocktail lounge, however. It's pronounced *Shy Shy* and named after a place in the nation of Mozambique, a former Portuguese colony.

Phone: +27 11 482 6990
Address: 7th Street, between 1st & 2nd avenues, Melville
Coordinates: 26°10'39.55"S
28° 0'30.61"E. (Coordinates in Google Earth are wrong).

Rodizio ☺☺☺☺☺ — Brazilian Portuguese. They have little coloured wooden semaphores on the tables, which are used to tell the waiters if you want more from the carvery or not. They also do Latin dancing.

Phone: +27 11 455 1093
Address: Shop 35, Village View Shopping Centre, Van Buuren Road, Bedfordview
Web: www.rodizio.co.za
Coordinates: 26°10'59.16"S,
28° 8'7.49"E

Steakhouses, Burgers, Bistros, and A la Carte

Baglio's ☺☺☺☺ — An a-la-carte restaurant featuring a wide variety of foods, especially steaks and pastas. They have an excellent ice-cream parlour.
Phone: +27 11 784 0105
Address: 5th Street, Nelson Mandela Square, Sandton
Coordinates: 26° 6'26.81"S
 28° 3'15.76"E

Browns ☺☺☺☺☺ — A la carte. Excellent food, albeit pricy. Very large wine collection.

Phone: +27 11 803 7533
Address: 21 Wessels Road, Rivonia
Web: www.browns.co.za
Coordinates: 26° 2'26.05"S,
26° 2'26.05"S (approximate).

The Butcher Shop and Grill ☺☺☺☺☺ — A restaurant for carnivores. Mainly steaks and grills. Very pricy.

Phone: +27 11 784 8676
Address: 5th Street, Nelson Mandela Square, Sandton
Web: www.thebutchershop.co.za
Coordinates: 26° 6'26.81"S
 28° 3'15.76"E

The Doll House — The only true roadhouse in central Johannesburg, this long-standing establishment is an institution. I can't vouch for its quality (good or bad), however.

Phone: +27 11 786 4703
Address: 377 Louis Botha Ave, Highlands North

Coordinates: 26° 8'51.98"S,
28° 5'10.82"E

Gourmet Garage ⊙⊙⊙⊙ — A franchise.
Big freshly-made burger patties. Home
of the Champagne Burger. Roadside
Diner food. Vegetarian burgers
available.

Phone: +27 11 511 0523
Address: Shop 64, Montecasino,
Montecasino Boulevard, Fourways.
Web: www.gourmetgarage.co.za
Coordinates: 26° 1'28.27"S
28° 0'45.61"E

The Grill House ⊙⊙⊙⊙⊙

Phone: +27 11 880 3945
Address: The Firs, 191 Oxford Rd,
Rosebank
Coordinates: 26° 8'36.65"S, 28° 2'36.50"E

The Meat Company — A franchise.
I recommend the branch at Monte
Casino or Melrose Arch. Best Steakhouse
award.
Web: www.themeatcompany.co.za

Monte Casino branch:
Phone: +27 11 511 0235
Address: Montecasino, Montecasino
Boulevard, Fourways.
Coordinates: 26° 1'28.27"S
28° 0'45.61"E

Melrose Arch branch:
Phone: +27 11 684 1787/8
Address: Melrose Square, High Street,
Melrose Arch, Athol Oaklands Road
Coordinates: 26° 8'2.18"S,
28° 4'5.24"E. (Google Earth has incorrect
coordinates. These are correct.)

Mike's Kitchen ⊙⊙⊙ — A magnificent
old Victorian house.

Phone: +27 11 484 2688
Address: 15 St Andrews Rd, Parktown
Web: www.mikeskitchen.co.za
Coordinates: 26°10'57.26"S,
28° 2'7.20"E

Smith and Wollensky ⊙⊙⊙⊙⊙ —
Excellent food and service. My personal
recommendation. A bit pricy.

Phone: +27 11 784 1437
Address: Upper Food Court, Eastgate
Shopping Centre, Nicol Rd., Bedfordview
Web: www.smithandwollensky.co.za
Coordinates: 26°10'49.06"S
26°10'49.06"S

Spur ⊙⊙⊙⊙ — The most popular
steakhouse franchise in South Africa.
Long queues and plenty of children, but
the food is pretty good. See their
website for a store locator.
Rosebank Branch: Texakhana Spur
Phone: +27 11 880 7158
Address: Shop FF02, The Zone, Oxford
Road, Rosebank
Coordinates: 26° 8'49.81"S
28° 2'33.19"E

Trump's Grill ⊙⊙⊙⊙ — Features a wide
variety of foods from all nations.

Phone: +27 11 784 2366
Address: 5th Street, Nelson Mandela
Square, Sandton
Coordinates: 26° 6'26.81"S, 28° 3'15.76"E

Turn 'n Tender — an old Jo'burg
stalwart that moved to the suburbs a
few years back.

Phone: +27 11 788 7933
Address: Cnr 7th Avenue & 3rd Street,
Parktown Quarter, Parktown North
Web: www.turnntender.co.za
Coordinates: 26° 8'41.46"S, 28° 1'44.06"E

The Westcliff Hotel — Superb views from the Westcliff Ridge, an old imperial hotel. It's frequented by the wealthiest people in Johannesburg and it is very busy, so you are advised to book a table in advance. Pricy.

Phone: +27 11 481 6000
Address: The Westcliff, 67 Jan Smuts Avenue, Westcliff
Web: www.westcliff.co.za
Coordinates: 26°10'14.32"S 28° 1'58.59"E (Google Earth has incorrect coordinates).

Wombles — Lunch and dinner Monday to Friday. Dinner only on Saturday. Closed Sunday. Highly rated.

Phone: +27 11 880 2470
Address: 17 3rd Avenue, Parktown North
Web: www.wombles.co.za
Coordinates: 26° 8'44.70"S 28° 1'43.14"E

Further Afield

Greensleeves Medieval Kingdom

⊚⊚⊚⊚ — A medieval-themed restaurant where you have to dress up in medieval garb. The food is medieval too — roasts on the spit, home-made bread, and mead. Be warned; there is a host who runs the party each night and he randomly selects people at the various tables to perform embarrassing tasks, such as karaoke. You also have to ask the "king" for salt. I imagine it is more fun when you're completely inebriated.
Phone: +27 83 229 5677 / +27 82 602 2958 (mobiles)
Address: R 563, Sterkfontein. Map on their website.
Web: www.greensleeves.co.za/joburg
Coordinates: 26° 1'54.08"S

27°43'2.33"E (their website gives different coordinates, you should phone and confirm).

The Carnivore — They stock all sorts of game, including crocodile. A must-see if you want to try different game meat. I suggest you go here for dinner after going to Sterkfontein Caves and Maropeng (see the chapter on Archaeology).

Phone: +27 11 950 6000
Address: 69 Drift Boulevard (R114), Muldersdrift (off Beyers Naudé drive, far north-west). Drift Boulevard is only 2km long so if you go further than that, you've gone too far.
Web: www.carnivore.co.za
Coordinates: 26° 1'43.96"S, 27°51'22.34"E (approximate).

Cornuti in the Cradle — A la carte, near Sterkfontein.

Phone: +27 11 659 1622
Address: Route T3, Kromdraai Rd, Kromdraai
Coordinates: 25°55'4.89"S, 27°50'49.02"E

Listings: Message to Restauranteurs

If you want to be listed here or improve your star ratings, contact me at *john@ostrowick.co.za*.

Appeal to Johannesburgers

If you know of an excellent restaurant that has been around for a few years which offers something unique (especially more Ethiopian places), please contact me at the above email address.

Chapter 9
Galleries

Introduction

Johannesburg has many small galleries scattered around the city. I will only list the main galleries. For more information, or to get a tour of the more edgy art venues around the city, see *http://www.art-tours.co.za*

In Johannesburg Itself

Everard Read Gallery — Also mainly local artists, very close to the Goodman Gallery.

Phone: +27 11 788 4805
Address: 6 Jellicoe Ave, Rosebank
Web: www.everard-read.co.za
Coordinates: 26° 8'35.65"S
28° 2'13.04"E

Goodman Gallery — Features local, emerging and established artists.

Phone: +27 11 788 1113
Address: 163 Jan Smuts Avenue, Parkwood, Johannesburg *or*
Arts on Main Precinct, Corner Main and Berea Streets, Johannesburg
Web: www.goodman-gallery.com
Coordinates: *Parkwood*: 26° 8'57.83"S
28° 2'1.63"E
Johannesburg CBD: 26°12'18.27"S
 28° 3'26.79"E

Johannesburg Art Gallery — Features local and international artists. A large historical collection.

Phone: +27 11 725 3130
Address: Cnr King George and Klein Street, Joubert Park
Coordinates: 26°11'49.88"S
28° 2'46.19"E

Standard Bank Gallery — Exhibitions are held here all year round, primarily of local artists.

Phone: +27 11 631 1889
Address: Corner Simmonds and Frederick Street, Johannesburg. Parking entrance in Harrison Street.
Web: www.standardbankarts.com
Coordinates: 26°12'35.88"S
28° 2'22.83"E

Further Afield

The Pretoria Art Museum

Situated in central Pretoria, this gallery easily rivals Johannesburg's collection. Worth a visit for all art lovers.

Phone: +27 12 344 1807/8
Address: Cnr Schoeman and Wessels Str, Arcadia Park, Arcadia, Pretoria
Web: www.pretoriaartmuseum.co.za
Coordinates: 25°44'54.64"S
28°12'49.39"E

More information

For more information see:

http://www.cultureclub.co.za/
http://www.art-tours.co.za

65

Chapter 10
Nightlife — Bars, Nightclubs and Theatres

Introduction

Johannesburg has a rich selection of nightclubs, bars, and live music venues, catering to every taste.

Some clubs in Johannesburg turn a blind eye towards smoking, but legally, you are not permitted at all to smoke in any public place. Venue owners can be fined up to R 10 000 for each violation so please rather assume that you may not smoke.

Most of the establishments listed here are places that I have been to or that are near tourist areas, but there are dozens more around the city, too many to list.

Please be aware that most nightclubs charge a "cover charge" before they will grant you entrance, and many of them have strict dress codes. You should check the website of each club for more information.

If you are interested in pubs, there aren't many in Johannesburg; most pubs double as restaurants, and vice versa. See the chapter on restaurants for details of *News Café, Q.Ba, Keg* and *Dros*. These franchises represent the majority of cocktail bars and pubs in Johannesburg, and they can be found in or near most malls.

I have also listed the major theatres in the city in this chapter. Most of the shows that are put on are worth going to see.

More comprehensive information can be found on *http://www.jhblive.com/* and *http://www.joburg.org.za/content/view/148/52/*. If you want to find out what's going on in Soweto, see *http://www.sowetolive.com/*

Warnings

Some bouncers and patrons can be unduly aggressive. You are advised to be cautious and avoid interactions which may cause trouble. I have omitted to mention venues here if they have had a bad reputation at some stage.

As a woman, take precautions in all clubs and bars against drink spiking. Do not leave your drink unattended and do not take a drink from a stranger directly; trust only the bar staff.

Pub / Cocktail Lounge Franchises

You can find the addresses of all these places on their websites. They are all wide-spread franchises.

Pubs:
Dros — www.dros.co.za
Keg — www.atthekeg.co.za
Stones — www.stones.co.za

Cocktail lounges:
News Café — www.newscafe.co.za
Q.ba — www.qbacaffe.co.za

Nightclubs

As there are many nightclubs in the Greater Johannesburg Area, I have divided this section up by area.

The Near East Rand, Edenvale, Linksfield, Germiston

Afrodisiac — Attached to a plant nursery, acts as a nightclub at night and restaurant by day. Entrance — look for the fires on Linksfield Drive. Crowd usually early-mid 20s.

Phone: +27 11 443 9990

Address: Corner Club Street, Civin & Linksfield Drive, Linksfield
Web: www.theafrodisiac.co.za
Coordinates: 26° 8'54.92"S, 28° 7'32.14"E

Classic Corner Head Quarters (CCHQ) — CCHQ is my first choice for you. Exquisite décor, friendly environment. This former antique shop is a must-see; there is nothing that comes close. They have a variety of events happening all the time; it's best to join their Facebook group (CCHQ Massive) and see what is happening. They run Indie Rock, Gay/Lesbian, House/Rave, and Goth/Industrial/Heavy metal events. One of the party hosts, Dark_Noise, who run the alternative music events, have S&M shows in a room called "the Dungeon". The venue is very tolerant of most things (apart from fighting, vandalism and standing on furniture), so it is a great place to let your hair down. Crowd usually mid-20s to mid-30s.

Phone: +27 11 822 4271
Address: Corner Main and Violet, Fisher's Hill, Germiston.
Web: www.myspace.com/cchq
Coordinates: 26°10'58.19"S,28° 9'41.75"E

The Doors — Long-standing club. Heavy metal, rock and alternative. They have strict behaviour policies and zealous bouncers. Young crowd.

Phone: +27 11 453 7673
Address: 19 Van Riebeeck Ave, Edenvale
Coordinates: 26° 8'54.10"S
28° 9'24.27"E

Ramp Divas — Gay club.

Address: 154 Annabella RD, Bardene. Turn right at Hyundai in North Rand Road. Boksburg.
Phone: +27 82 680 3691/ 82 932 2161
Web: www.rampdivas.co.za
Coordinates: 26°10'30.95"S
28°14'29.20"E (approximate).

Stones Edenvale — Radio-friendly pop, house, R&B/hip-hop. Sometimes have rock events. A bit on the macho side. A franchise, widespread.

Phone: +27 11 609 5437
Address: Edenmeadow Shopping Centre, Cnr Modderfontein Rd and Van Riebeeck Avenue, Edenvale
Web: www.stones.co.za
Coordinates: 26° 7'13.84"S,
28° 8'17.56"E

Johannesburg CBD and Newtown

Bassline — If you want an African experience, I'd say this is the place for you, or **Kippies**, which is nearby.
Phone: +27 11 838 9145
Address: 10 Henry Nxumalo Street, Newtown
Web: www.bassline.co.za
Coordinates: 26°12'19.26"S
28° 1'53.64"E

Carfax — House and R&B. Their venue hosts a variety of events and you should check their website. Younger crowd.

Phone: +27 11 834 9187
Address: 39 Pim Street, Newtown. (Google Earth has another name for the street).
Web: www.carfax.co.za (website may have a problem)
Coordinates: 26°12'4.65"S,
28° 1'43.61"E

Go-Go Bar — Electro and Hip Hop. Fri-Sat only.

Phone: +27 83 419 5912 (mobile)
Address: Corner of Bree and Henry Nxumalo streets, Newtown
Coordinates: 26°12'7.82"S
28° 1'50.29"E

Kippies Jazz club — The iconic Jazz club of Johannesburg, named for the famous musician Kippie Moeketsi, who like many African artists, died destitute. A must-see for tourists. It was closed for a number of years due to structural problems with the building. It has now been re-opened.

Address: 56 Margaret Mcingana Street (previously Wolhuter), Newtown
Web: www.markettheatre.co.za
Coordinates: 26°12'4.89"S
28° 1'56.62"E

The Men Factory (Gay club) — House and electro.

Phone: +27 83 965 2227 (mobile)
Address: 6 6th Street, New Doornfontein
Web: www.thefactorybar.co.za
Coordinates: 26°11'56.43"S 28° 3'46.98"E

Simply Blue (Gay club) — Bar by day and club by night.

Phone: +27 82 876 8976 (mobile)
Address: 90 De Korte Street, Braamfontein
Web: www.clubsimplyblue.com
Coordinates: 26°11'36.94"S 28° 2'9.56"E (approximate)

Melville and Nearby Suburbs

Back2Basix — A live music venue, but they also serve food.

Phone: +27 11 726 6857
Address: 167 Perth Rd, Westdene Corner Kingsway and Lancaster Road
Web: back2basix.co.za
Coordinates: 26°10'51.81"S 27°59'42.56"E

The Bohemian — An arty hangout, by reputation.

Phone: 011 482 1725
Address: 5 Park Road, Richmond
Web: www.thebo.co.za
Coordinates: 26°10'54.79"S,28° 0'50.20"E

Catz Pyjamas — A nightclub and tapas restaurant. Early to Mid-twenties crowd.

Phone: +27 11 726 8596
Address: 12 Main Rd (University Drive), Melville
Web: www.catzpyjamas.co.za
Coordinates: 26°10'37.86"S 28° 0'4.13"E

Cool Runnings — Primarily a restaurant or bar, they play Reggae only and serve Jamaican food. They also sometimes have shows in their "dungeon".

Phone: +27 11 482 4786
Address: 27 4th Avenue, Melville
Web: www.coolrunnings.co.za
Coordinates: 26°10'35.35"S, 28° 0'4.83"E

ESP — Rave. Saturdays only.

Address: 84 Oxford Street, Ferndale, Randburg.
Web: www.esp.co.za
http://www.facebook.com/group.php?gid=2486755068
Coordinates: 26° 4'50.74"S 27°59'17.78"E (approximate).

Roka — A wide range of music, differing every night; mostly house, R&B, but Tuesday is rock. Also a cocktail lounge.

Phone: +27 11 482 2023
Address: 44 Stanley Avenue, Milpark
Web: www.rokalounge.com
Coordinates: 26°11'6.53"S 28° 1'9.02"E

Roxy's Rhythm Bar — Johannesburg's oldest nightclub. Generally a live music venue, usually plays house or rock. Younger crowd.

Phone: +27 11 726 6019
Address: 20 Main Rd, Melville
Web: www.clubroxy.co.za
Coordinates: 26°10'34.37"S
28° 0'3.14"E

Venus Fly Trap/Rascasse

Formerly part of *Roxy's*, this club (upstairs) plays R&B. Younger crowd. Cocktail lounge is downstairs. Details and location as per Roxy's.

Stones Melville

Phone: +27 11 726 1683
Address: 7 Main Rd, Melville
Web: www.stones.co.za
Coordinates: 26°10'36.23"S,
28° 0'3.75"E

North West

The Coca Cola Dome, Northgate Shopping Centre. All international music acts play here.

Ninety Six — Lounge.

Phone: +2711 467 6696

Address: Corner Witkoppen and Main Roads, Fourways.
Web: www.ninetysix.co.za
Coordinates: 26° 1'39.52"S
28° 1'45.12"E

Red Room — Indie rock, alternative. Pretty far from anywhere in Johannesburg. Tiny, but worth seeing for its red and mirrored walls. Good music. DJ Ashton is also lead singer in an SA Goth band (The Awakening). Drive north up Beyers Naudé drive for about 5.7km after the motorway ("western bypass") offramp. Look out on your left for Juice street and the sign saying "Le Club". Only open on Saturday night, 10 PM onwards. Similar music to The Doors nightclub but an older clientele.

Address: Corner Beyers Naudé and Juice Street, Laser Park
Web: www.redroom.co.za
Coordinates: 26° 4'29.12"S,
27°55'12.45"E

Sandton, Central, Northern Suburbs

Blues Room — A bar, more than a club. They generally have live acts.

Phone: +27 11 838 9145 / 784 5527
Address: Shop L8, Village Walk, cnr Rivonia and Maude Street, Sandton

70

Web: www.bluesroom.co.za
Coordinates: 26° 6'13.13"S, 28° 3'35.71"E

The Crazy 88 — Indie rock and other genres.

Phone: +27 11 728 8417
Address: 114 William Road, cnr Grant Ave, Norwood
Web: www.88.co.za
Coordinates: 26° 9'27.98"S 28° 4'33.46"E (approximate)

The Jolly Roger — A famous pub. Good pizza.

Phone: +27 11 442 3954
Address: 10 4th Avenue, Parkhurst.
Coordinates: 26° 8'33.47"S, 28° 1'0.69"E

Katzy's at the Grillhouse — Blues, modeled on a cigar lounge style.
Phone: +27 11 880 3945
Address: The Firs, Oxford Road, Rosebank
Web: www.thegrillhouse.co.za
Coordinates: 26° 8'37.91"S 28° 2'36.70"E

The Radium Beer Hall — A long-standing pub (dating back to 1929). The Radium has a very long history of association with Johannesburg's troubled past. They feature live bands most nights and have a typical pub menu. The music tends to be blues, jazz and rock. A must-see.
　　　　Be aware that parking on Louis Botha is a chancy business. Try to park near the pub, and be generous to your parking attendant.

Phone: +27 11 728 3866
Address: 282 Louis Botha Avenue, Orange Grove
Web: www.theradium.co.za

Coordinates: 26° 9'45.79"S 28° 5'2.65"E

Taboo — Situated in upmarket Sandton, they play house and R&B. Right near News Café, if you want to go somewhere else nearby.

Phone: +27 11 783 2200
Address: 24 Central, Cnr Fredman Drive and Gwen Lane, Sandton
Web: www.taboo.co.za
Coordinates: 26° 6'9.35"S 28° 3'24.60"E

Tanz Café — A comedy dinner club and dance venue, with live music. Closed Sunday and Monday.

Phone: +27 11 463 3128/ 5937
Address: The River Road, cnr Bryanston Drive, Riverside
Web: www.tanzcafe.co.za
Coordinates: 26° 4'9.03"S, 28° 2'17.89"E

Strip Clubs

We have three main strip clubs in Jo'burg (Sandton area): *The Grand*, *Lollipop Lounge* and *Teazers*. They're quite expensive, aimed at an upmarket crowd, and generally offer an a-la-carte menu, too. I've not visited them myself (really) but I understand they require a dress code — collar and tie, jacket required. I leave it up to you to find them. You are advised to not go to any other strip joints than these three. Remember that you must not touch the performers.

Soweto

Soweto's club culture is a recent development; traditionally, nightlife in Soweto consisted of a visit to the local shebeen, of which there are plenty.

71

DJ's Bar Lounge — Live music and African food.

Phone: +27 11 935 7460
Address: 1198 Ngculu St, Orlando East, Soweto
Coordinates: 26°14'24.94"S 27°55'29.53"E (approximate, call for directions).

The Rock — DJs and African music.

Phone: +27 11 986 8182
Address: 1987 Vundla St, Rockville, Soweto
Web: www.therock.co.za
Coordinates: 26°15'54.36"S 27°52'20.14"E

Theatres

In this section I will simply document live theatres, not movie theatres, as the latter can be found in any mall (see the chapter on shopping).

The Civic Theatre / Johannesburg Theatre — This theatre tends to put on classic productions, such as Shakespeare or Broadway. At the end of every year they put on a pantomime.

Phone: +27 11 877 6800
Address: 158 Loveday Street, Braamfontein
Web: www.showbusiness.co.za
Coordinates: 26°11'26.73"S, 28° 2'22.58"E

The Market Theatre — Primarily arty and politically-oriented intellectual shows are put on here.

Phone: +27 11 832 1641
Address: 56 Margaret Mcingana Street (formerly Wolhuter), Newtown
Web: www.markettheatre.co.za
Coordinates: 26°12'6.72"S, 28° 1'56.76"E

The Teatro at Monte Casino — They seem to put more popular shows on here, such as musicals, extravaganzas and feat shows.

Phone: +27 11 511 1988
Address: Wiliam Nicol Drive, Monte Casino, Fourways/Magaliessig
Web: www.montecasinotheatre.co.za
Coordinates: 26° 1'28.60"S 28° 0'53.52"E

Theatre on the Square — Located at Nelson Mandela Square, this theatre is primarily convenient if you're staying at the Michelangelo Hotel or going to dinner at one of the restaurants on the square.

Phone: +27 11 883 8606
Address: Nelson Mandela Square, 5th Street, Sandton
Web: www.at.artslink.co.za/~tots/
Coordinates: 26° 6'26.81"S
28° 3'15.76"E

Victory Theatre — Dating back to the 1920s, this theatre mainly shows musicals, pantomimes, and local productions. *Afrika Umoja* is their flagship show.

Phone: +27 11 728 9603
Address: Corner Osborne Rd and Louis Botha Avenue, Orange Grove
Web: www.victorytheatre.co.za
Coordinates: 26°10'5.88"S
28° 4'36.36"E

Wits University Theatre
Primarily intended as a theatre for the University's Drama department. Some classics have been shown here and there is almost always a Shakespeare shown every year.

Phone: + 27 11 717 1111
Address: Cnr Station and Jorrissen Streets, Braamfontein
Web: web.wits.ac.za/placesofinterest/witstheatre
Coordinates: 26°11'34.62"S
28° 1'56.32"E

Wits University, Linder Auditorium — The National Symphony Orchestra sometimes performs here.

Address: Wits Education Campus, 27 St Andrews Road, Parktown.
Coordinates: 26°10'42.55"S
28° 2'32.72"E

Further Afield

The State Theatre, Pretoria — the main theatre in the country. All major shows are put on here.
Phone: +27 12 392 4000
Address: 320 Pretorius Street, Cnr Prinsloo, Pretorius and Van Der Walt Streets, Pretoria
Web: www.statetheatre.co.za
Coordinates: 25°44'50.75"S
25°44'50.75"S

Message to Club/Bar/Theatre Owners

If you own a nightclub or theatre and want to be listed here, or if you want to have some information here altered, please contact me at:
john@ostrowick.co.za.

Chapter 11
Sports

Introduction

South Africans are completely mad about sport, so you can expect to find many sport clubs and venues in and around Johannesburg.

This chapter lists only a few that are open to the public, or that may have a tournament of some sort on that you may be able to go and see. To a large extent, many sports clubs are private, so you will have to call and enquire before showing up.

Some sporting events take place in Pretoria, most notably, Rugby (at Loftus Versveld), however, there is a new soccer stadium as well, specifically for the 2010 Soccer World Cup™.

There are also many tourist-oriented sports and outdoor activities available in Johannesburg. I will list them under an "Activities" subheading.

Stadiums

Ellis Park — there are actually two stadiums in Ellis Park; used for track and field events as well as soccer. Sometimes these stadiums are also used for rock concerts.

Phone: +27 11 402 8644
Address: 48 Staib Street, Doornfontein
Web: www.ellispark.co.za
Coordinates: 26°11'44.45"S
28° 3'43.13"E

Soccer City — newly-built for the Fifa™ Soccer World Cup™. A dramatic sight, based on the design of an African basket. Seats almost 100 000 people.

Phone: +27 11 494 3640
Address: Nasrec Rd, Nasrec,
Web: www.soccercity2010.co.za
Coordinates: 26°14'7.56"S
26°14'7.56"S

Wanderers Cricket Stadium — the historic world-famous cricket grounds. There is a golf course there too.

Phone: +27 11 340 1500
Address: Corlett Drive, Illovo
Web: www.wanderers.co.za
Coordinates: 26° 7'52.29"S
28° 3'25.85"E

Racecourses and Motor Racing

Kyalami Race Track — the famous international motor racing track.

Phone: +27 11 466 2800
Address: Kyalami Grand Prix Circuit 1, Allendale Road, Kyalami, Midrand
Web: www.kyalamiracing.co.za
Coordinates: 25°59'48.84"S 28° 4'10.00"E

Turffontein Racecourse — horse racing. Restaurant on-site. The original Johannesburg racecourse.

Phone: +27 11 681 1899
Address: Turf Club Street, La Rochelle Rd/Rosettenville Rd, Turffontein, Johannesburg
Web: www.phumelela.co.za
Coordinates: 26°14'14.59"S 28° 2'44.41"E

Newmarket Racecourse — horse racing. Sometimes hosts concerts.

Phone: +27 11 907 9753
Address: Cnr Heidelberg & Ring Road East, Alberton, Johannesburg
Web: http://www.southafrica.info/about/sport/horseracing.htm
Coordinates: 26°16'31.12"S 28° 7'32.88"E

Golf Courses

Johannesburg has no shortage of golf courses. Just within or adjacent to the central N1/N12/N3 ring road I count nine, in alphabetic order:

Glendower — Phone: +27 11 453 1013. Address: 2 Marais Road, Dowerglen, Edenvale. Web: www.glendower.co.za. Coordinates: 26° 9'37.20"S, 28° 8'30.44"E. A small course.

Golf Village Driving Range — Phone: +27 11 622 4442. Address: 47 Boeing Road West, Bedfordview. Web: http://www.vgolfv.co.za/gilloolys.asp. Coordinates: 26°10'17.57"S, 28° 7'43.29"E. Just a driving range.

Houghton Golf Club — Phone: +27 11 728 7337. Address: 2nd Avenue, Lower Houghton. Coordinates: 26° 9'52.11"S, 28° 4'11.65"E. A very famous course.

Johannesburg Country Club — Phone: +27 11 710 6400. Address: 1 Napier Rd, Auckland Park. Web: www.ccj.co.za. Coordinates: 26°10'59.58"S, 26°10'59.58"S. A small course.

Killarney Country Club — Phone: +27 11 442 7411. Address: 5th Street, Killarney. Web: www.killarneycountryclub.co.za. Coordinates: 26° 9'6.87"S, 26° 9'6.87"S. They offer other sports. Very exclusive.

Linksfield Golf Course — Phone: +27 11 640 5762. Address: 119 Club Street, Linksfield. Website: www.linksfield.co.za. Coordinates: 26° 9'22.41"S, 28° 7'12.10"E. Probably the largest course in Jo'burg.

Observatory Golf Club and Driving Range — Phone: +27 11 487 3898/ +27 11 648 9579. Address: 5 Steyn Street, Observatory. Web: www.observatorygolfclub.co.za. Coordinates: 26°10'43.59"S, 28° 4'41.47"E.

Parkview Golf Course — Phone: +27 11 646 5725/5400. Address: Cnr Wickow Ave & Emmarentia Ave. Coordinates: 26° 9'41.09"S, 28° 1'10.36"E. One of the oldest clubs in Jo'burg.

The River Country Club — Phone: +27 11 783 1166. Address: Links Rd, Sandton. Coordinates: 26° 4'39.38"S, 28° 2'14.13"E.

Wanderers Golf Club — Phone: +27 11 447 3311. Address: Corlett Drive, Illovo. Web: Coordinates: 26° 8'2.59"S, 28° 3'7.64"E.

Other Activities

There are many outdoor activities you can engage in within Johannesburg. Walks and parks will be listed in a later chapter.

Cycling — One of the main sporting events in Johannesburg, which blocks up a good portion of the main roads, is the *Momentum/94.7 Cycle Challenge*. It involves cycling around almost the entire central part of the city.

Phone: +27 11 463 2743
Address: 3 East River Road West, Bryanston
Web: www.cyclechallenge.co.za

It is an annual event, occurring in November.

Hot Air Ballooning —
www.balloon.co.za
www.discoverballooning.co.za
www.hotairballooningsa.co.za

For the most part, these companies operate just outside of Johannesburg, near Hartebeespoort Dam, about an hour's drive north. The exception is at Gold Reef City, where they also offer a hot air balloon ride.

Skydiving —
www.jsc.co.za
www.icarus.co.za
www.skyhightandems.co.za

Bungee Jumping —
www.orlandotowers.co.za

Rock climbing —
www.adventureescapades.co.za
www.ventureforth.co.za
www.climb.co.za

There are plenty of other offerings in Johannesburg: go-karting, ten-pin bowling, indoor soccer, indoor cricket, bowls, etc. See *http://www.jozikids.co.za/johannesburg/to_go/action/indoors/* for more.

76

Chapter 12
Theme Parks and Casinos

Introduction

There are a number of theme parks and casinos in the Johannesburg area; I've only listed the large, reputable ones.

Emperor's Palace Casino — East Rand, right next door to OR Tambo airport. They feature a wide range of dining and entertainment options, including shows, a club, a bar, and a theatre. Like Monte Casino and Gold Reef City, there is a hotel attached to this casino.

Phone: +27 11 928 1000
Address: 64 Jones Road, Kempton Park
Web: www.emperorspalace.co.za
Coordinates: 26° 8'44.61"S 28°13'17.15"E

Gold Reef City — An authentic Victorian town. It showcases life in the gold rush days of Johannesburg. You can go down a mine shaft, and watch a gold bar being cast. There is also a casino and amusement park.

Phone: +27 11 248-6800 and +27 11 248 6896
Address: Follow Alamein/Northern Parkway Road and Gold Reef Road, Ormonde
Web: www.goldreefcity.co.za
Coordinates: 26°14'14.87"S 28° 0'53.16"E

Monte Casino — A faux village styled along Italian Tuscan design.

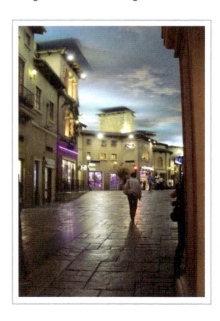

They have many restaurants and a gigantic movie theatre. Worth seeing for its kitsch decor and fake indoor sky alone. You may not take photographs at the casino itself. They also have a bird park.

Address: Cnr William Nicol and Montecasino Boulevard, Fourways
Web: www.montecasino.co.za
Coordinates: 26° 1'28.27"S, 28° 0'45.61"E

Santarama and Miniland, Wemmer Pan — A lake with a theme park on its coast featuring miniature models of significant buildings in Johannesburg. I understand it is being upgraded because it fell into disrepair.

Phone: +27 11 435 0543
Address: Wemmer Pan Road/180 Rosettenville Road, near the Wemmer Pan lake itself.
Web: http://www.joburg.org.za/content/view/358/52/
Coordinates: 26°13'51.43"S 28° 3'31.04"E (Approximate, look out for brown signs)

Wild Waters — A water theme park with various slides and a wave tank. It operates a night club, *H2O*, on some weekend nights. It does not have a casino.

Address: Rondebult Rd offramp, Left into Cynthia Rd (parallel to North Rand Rd), Boksburg.
Coordinates: 26°10'30.47"S, 28°14'38.81"E

Further Afield

Sun City — The gambling Mecca of South Africa. It has a faux tropical palace for a hotel, a golf course, a fake beach with waves, a large casino, and many extravaganzas. There's something there for everyone. Highly recommended.

Sun City was originally placed that far out from Jo'burg because gambling was illegal in Apartheid South Africa, so only native African "homelands" were allowed to have casinos on them. Furthermore, international performers refused to come to South Africa, so since the "homelands" were technically separate countries, international acts would perform at Sun City.

Phone:+27 14 557 1000
Address: Sun City Resort, North West Province. Head North-west from William Nicol Drive and keep following the signs. See http://suncityhotels.co.za/directions.htm; approximately 120km from Johannesburg, 40km north of Rustenburg.
Web: www.suncity.co.za
Coordinates: 25°20'46.86"S 27° 5'56.82"E

As Sun City is a very large resort with many activities (not just a casino), and as it is quite far out, you should probably book in at one of their hotels to get the full benefit of all their offerings.

Chapter 13
Animals, Game Parks and Nature Reserves

Introduction

Johannesburg has a number of animal attractions and parks, either within its boundaries or nearby. If you're a keen birder, Johannesburg is a great place to visit; there are a fair number of native African species such as barbets, glossy starlings, weavers, bishops and turacos.

A Grey Loerie — a type of turaco.

Warning: Please be aware that the animals you're going to see are not tame and that you are placing yourself and your fellow passengers and tourists in extreme danger by getting out of your car in any area which is not clearly marked as safe for you to do so. Some tourists have, for example, been killed by lions. This applies equally to the animals in the zoo.

Within Johannesburg Itself

Parks and Nature Reserves

Johannesburg Botanical Gardens and Emmarentia Dam — There are a number of small lakes, a small stream, a massive park, and various fountains at this venue. There are many exotic plant species and an attractive rose garden. The dogs are very amusing. It's best in spring. It's very close to Greenside, where there are a variety of nice restaurants.

Phone: +27 11 782 7064
Address: Olifants Road, Emmarentia
Coordinates: 26° 9'8.23"S
28° 0'9.62"E

Linksfield Ridge — You can hike up Linksfield ridge (the Harvey Nature Reserve). Fantastic views of Johannesburg in every direction. It is fenced off on many sides so finding an entrance can be tricky. Don't go up alone, and if you see loiterers, leave. No interesting animals, just a view.

Address: Linksfield Ridge, Linksfield
Web: http://www.footprint.co.za/Linksfield_ridge.htm.
Coordinates: 26° 9'58.95"S 28° 7'6.53"E

Melville Koppies — another ridge of indigenous scrub land/veld. Has some archaeological remains. By appointment only.

Phone: +27 11 482 4797
Address: Judith Road, Melville
Web: www.mk.org.za
Coordinates: 26°10'15.67"S, 28° 0'20.66"E

Modderfontein Conservation Area — You can see guinea fowl and red bishops here (bird species). They also have a fish eagle. I was married here!

Address: Arden Rd., Modderfontein
Coordinates: 26° 3'48.84"S, 28° 7'23.44"E

Walter Sisulu Botanical Gardens — A beautiful koppie and waterfall is one of the chief features of these gardens. Apparently there is a nesting pair of eagles, and a variety of small wildlife.

Phone: 086 100 1278 (inside SA only)
Address: End of Malcolm Road, Poortview, Roodepoort
Web: www.sanbi.org
Coordinates: 26° 5'15.02"S, 27°50'42.01"E

Zoo Lake — Features local artists on a Sunday, and sometimes a craft market. Also has a branch of Moyo, the African restaurant. You can hire a boat and go rowing. Right near the Johannesburg Zoo and Military History Museum.

Address: 1 Prince of Wales Drive, Parkview
Web: http://www.footprint.co.za/zoo_lake.htm
Coordinates: 26° 9'26.63"S, 28° 1'46.18"E

Animal Attractions

Johannesburg Zoo

A very large zoo, dating back to 1904. It will easily take you a day to explore. You should make sure that you see the white lions, the big cat enclosure, and the birds of prey. They even have a polar bear.

The food and catering at the zoo is somewhat overpriced so you should consider bringing your own picnic. The zoo serves as an ecological research

centre and concentrates on making realistic environments for the animals. They are particularly focused on eliminating the old cages and replacing them with more suitable environments.
    They also do events at night, especially music and picnic events.

Phone: +27 11 646 2000
Address: Upper Park Drive, Forest Town/Saxonwold
Web: www.jhbzoo.org.za
Coordinates: 26°10'9.72"S 28° 2'14.80"E

The Lion Park — Do not leave your car under any circumstances. This is where the aforementioned tourists were killed. A wide variety of animals can be seen here including black leopards.

Phone: +27 11 460 1814
Address: Cnr Malibongwe Rd & R114, Honeydew, Randburg
Coordinates: 25°59'35.10"S, 27°55'47.91"E

Monte Casino Bird Gardens — This small park also has snakes from the old Transvaal Snake Park that used to be in Midrand.

Phone: +27 11 511 1864
Address: Montecasino Boulevard, Cnr William Nicol and Witkoppen Rds, Fourways
Web: http://www.montecasino.co.za/entertainment/family/Bird%20Gardens/Pages/default.aspx
Coordinates: 26° 1'22.14"S 28° 0'38.48"E

Rhino Lion Nature Reserve — This reserve is just within sight of Johannesburg's outer limits.

Many tourists come to South Africa to see Cape Town, and then promptly fly via Johannesburg to the Kruger Park. In so doing, these tourists risk missing out on seeing a number of wild animals, as the parks around Jo'burg are smaller, and therefore not only easier to explore without a guide, but also afford you a much higher probability of seeing something. In fact, I guarantee that you will see at least two or three of the Big Five at the Rhino Lion Park, amongst many other animals.

There is also a small petting zoo and breeding area, which includes a number of rare species such as tigers and jaguars. You can play with the lion cubs.
    They also have accommodation at this reserve, so you can stay over if you want to. Personally, I found that a full day there was enough.

The Rhino Lion Reserve also contains the *Wonder Cave* mentioned in the section on archaeology, and a vulture feeding area. I'd say if you choose one animal attraction, choose this.

Phone: +27 11 957 0349 / 0106 / 0109
Address: R28/N14, Main Rd off Kromdraai Rd, Kromdraai/Sterkfontein
Web: www.rhinolion.co.za
Coordinates: 25°58'24.50"S 27°47'34.51"E

Further Afield

Askari Lodge and Plumari Reserve

They have the Big Five at this reserve.

Phone: +27 14 577-2658/9
Address: Go from Roodepoort Past Krugersdorp up Rustenberg Rd. At Cnr R560 (Rustenberg Rd) and Doornhoek Rd, turn right into Doornhoek. 3.8km down the road is another road, turn left. Go 5km up that road. You should be there.
Web: www.askarilodge.co.za
Coordinates: 25°53'28.79"S 27°30'10.59"E (the coordinates on their website differ markedly. Consult their website for the map).

De Wildt Cheetah Centre

You can play with cheetah cubs here, and see adults. About 70km out of Johannesburg, or about two hours' drive, De Wildt is around the corner from Hartebeespoort Dam, on the other side of Pretoria in the opposite direction of the way to Rustenburg/Brits.

Phone: +27 12-5049906 / 7 / 8
Address: 3km eastwards down Brits Road, off the R514, about 8km north east of Hartebeespoort Dam as the crow flies.
Web: www.dewildt.co.za
Coordinates: 25°40'39.35"S 27°55'19.88"E (Google Earth has incorrect coordinates)

Hartebeespoort Dam

A popular destination for Jo'burgers wanting to go sit on a lake with a boat, but who don't want to travel too far. There is a flea market there, a snake park, hot air ballooning, and plenty of places to eat. You might want to check in at a hotel as the travel time to and from Jo'burg wastes a day.

Address: 32km north of Fourways.
Web: www.hartbeespoortdam.com
www.hartbeespoortsnakeanimalpark.co.za
Coordinates: 25°43'31.58"S 27°50'50.79"E (to the tunnel). Waterfront street: 25°43'49.41"S, 27°51'54.24"E

Loskop Dam Nature Reserve — Loskop Dam is 27km long and occupies 23 square kilometers. The nature reserve around it is even bigger.

Phone: +27 0 13 262 3075/6/7 (Resort)
Address: Take the R22 from Johannesburg to Witbank. Pass the Ultra City and take the Van Dijksdrif / Middelburg West off ramp. Turn left towards Middelburg on the R575, at the T-junction turn right into the R555, which becomes the N11. Follow the road for 50km to the Resort.
Web: www.loskopcountry.co.za (one of the resorts).
Coordinates: 25°25'30.02"S, 29°23'3.46"E

Pretoria Zoo — Many people who visit this zoo say that it is superior to Johannesburg's. Dates back to 1899. This zoo also has a highly-regarded night tour, and features Australian animals. They also have a cable car.

Phone: +27 12 328 3265
Address: 232 Boom Street, Pretoria (cnr Paul Kruger and Boom).
Web: www.zoo.ac.za

Coordinates: 25°44'19.61"S 28°11'19.34"E

Suikerbosrand — Has wild animals and accommodation. Mostly hiking though.

Phone: +27 0 11 904-3930 / 3 / 7
Address: Follow Heidelberg Rd south. At Alberton Road/Klipriver Road, turn right (west). Follow Alberton Rd for 6km. Turn left into Suikerbosrand Rd. It's 24km south of Rand Airport, Germiston, as the crow flies.
Web: http://www.gauteng.com/content.php?page=Suikerbosrand%20Nature%20Reserve
Coordinates: 26°28'53.44"S 28°12'41.35"E

Vaal Dam — The Vaal Dam is massive. It collects water from the Vaal River and supplies it to Johannesburg. The river serves as a border for Gauteng. The dam is over 300 square kilometres in size. It also has its own island. Many world-class boating events take place here.

Phone: +27 11 454 2520
Address: N3 south to Deneysville, approximately 85km directly south of Johannesburg..
Web: www.vaaldam.co.za
Coordinates: 26°53'23.56"S, 28° 5'47.87"E

83

Chapter 15
Accommodation

Introduction

There are probably hundreds of hotels in Johannesburg. I will list only the main ones. You can find more on the web.

You should choose your hotel based on its proximity to the sights you want to see as well as whether they offer transport or parking within the hotel grounds; avoid taking any accommodation in Jo'burg where you have to park in the street, as your car will likely be tampered with.

I do not recommend that you stay at a hotel in the old CBD anymore, as it is very run-down. You should try to take accommodation in the Central/Parks/Rosebank[1] areas, Sandton/Rivonia areas or near the Airport — Sandton because of its proximity to high-quality stores, malls and restaurants, the Central/Rosebank/Parks areas because of their proximity to tourist attractions, and the airport is good as well because it's on a motorway and it will ensure that you catch your flight on time!

The star ratings given for each hotel below are the *Tourism Grading Council star ratings, not my own*. If the gradings are not listed, it's because the hotels didn't advertise their gradings. Most hotels are 3-5 stars in Jo'burg. If you think my recommendations are too expensive, more hotels can

be found online at *http://johannesburg.hotelguide.co.za* and *http://sandton.hotelguide.co.za*.

There is a very cheap hotel chain called *Formula 1* that is found all over South Africa. Their website is *www.hotelformula1.co.za*. I suspect they're only two or three stars. *Holiday Inn* have many branches with various grades: *www.holidayinn.co.za*. *City Lodge*, *www.citylodge.co.za*, are also widespread.

Incidentally, I find that most South African companies ignore email (especially big companies), so it's best to do bookings over the phone or on the hotel websites.

Hotels

Sandton

The Balalaika. ⊚⊚⊚⊚ — Phone: +27 11 322 5000. Address: 90 Maude Street. Web: www.balalaika.co.za. Coordinates: 26° 6'16.67"S, 28° 3'31.61"E.

City Lodge. ⊚⊚⊚ — Phone: +27 11 444-5300. Address: Cnr Katherine Str & Grayston Drive. Web: www.citylodge.co.za, www.citylodge-katherinestreet.co.za. Coordinates: 26° 6'13.34"S, 28° 4'13.34"E.

---

[1] "The Parks" are the central suburbs with "Park" in their name.

Don Suites. ⊚⊚⊚⊚ — Phone: +27 11 709 1900. Address: 115 Pretoria Avenue, cnr Stella. Coordinates: 26° 6'25.31"S, 26° 6'25.31"S (approximate). Right near Gautrain station. There is also 125 Pretoria Street and 3 Rivonia Rd. Web: Web: www.don.co.za/Sandton_hotels

The Hilton. ⊚⊚⊚⊚⊚ — Phone: +27 11 322 1888. Address: 138 Rivonia Rd. Web: http://www1.hilton.com/en_US/hi/hotel/JNBSATW-Hilton-Sandton/index.do. Coordinates: 26° 6'5.18"S, 28° 3'35.59"E.

Holiday Inn. ⊚⊚⊚⊚ — Phone: +27 11 282 0000. Address: 123 Rivonia Rd. Web: hisandton.co.za. Coordinates: 26° 6'15.55"S, 28° 3'35.75"E.

The Michelangelo. ⊚⊚⊚⊚⊚ — Phone: +27 11 282 7000. Address: 135 West Street, Nelson Mandela Square. Web: www.michelangelo.co.za. Coordinates: 26° 6'25.04"S, 28° 3'23.82"E.

The Radisson. — A brand-new skyscraper in Sandton. Phone:+27 11 286 1000. Address: Corner Rivonia Rd and West Street. Web: www.radissonblu.com/hotelsandton-johannesburg. Coordinates: 26° 6'28.76"S, 26° 6'28.76"S.

Sandton Sun. ⊚⊚⊚⊚⊚ — Phone: +27 11 780 5000. Address: Cnr 5th & Alice Streets. Web: www.southernsun.com. Coordinates: 26° 6'25.10"S, 28° 3'6.18"E.

The Saxon. ⊚⊚⊚⊚⊚ — Phone: +27 11 292 6000. Address: 36 Saxon Rd. Web: www.thesaxon.com. Coordinates: 26° 6'43.63"S, 28° 2'8.20"E.

Southern Sun Grayston Drive. ⊚⊚⊚⊚ — Phone: +27 11 783 5262. Address: Cnr. Rivonia Road & Grayston Drive Sandton. Web: www.southernsun.com. Coordinates: 26° 5'54.82"S, 26° 5'54.82"S.

Southern Sun Katherine Street. ⊚⊚⊚⊚ — Phone: +27 11 884 8544. Address: 115 Katherine Street. Web: www.southernsun.com. Coordinates: 26° 6'21.83"S, 28° 3'57.04"E (approximate).

Holiday Inn Express. — Phone: +27 11 260 4000. Address: 54 Maxwell Drive, Woodmead. Web: www.holidayinn.co.za. Coordinates: 26° 2'34.71"S, 28° 5'49.86"E (approximate).

Holiday Inn Intercontinental, Sandton Towers. — Phone: +27 11 780 5555. Address: Corner Of Maude & 5th Streets. Web: www.holidayinn.co.za. Coordinates: 26° 6'26.58"S, 28° 3'11.45"E.

Far north

Kyalami Castle. Very novel, half-way between Pretoria and Johannesburg, near the motorway to the airport. Currently the headquarters of the Church of Scientology, but you can still stay there. Right near the racetrack.

Phone: +27 11 799 7676
Address: 66 Pine Avenue, Kyalami
Web: www.castlekyalami.com
Coordinates: 25°59'53.91"S
25°59'53.91"S

Rosebank, Central and Parks

Crowne Plaza Hotel Holiday Inn. —
Phone: +27 11 448 3600
Address: Cnr Tyrwhitt And Sturdee Avenues, Rosebank
Web: www.holidayinn.co.za.
Coordinates: 26° 8'44.85"S, 28° 2'18.53"E.

Don Suites. ⓞⓞⓞⓞ — Phone: +27 11 880 1666. Address: 10 Tyrwhitt Avenue. Web: www.don.co.za. Coordinates: 26° 8'44.85"S, 28° 2'18.53"E.

The Grace. ⓞⓞⓞⓞⓞ — Phone: +27 11 280 7200. Address: 54 Bath Avenue. Web: africansunhotels.com. Coordinates: 26° 8'43.67"S, 28° 2'26.73"E.

Holiday Inn : Rosebank The Zone. —
Phone: +27 11 218 6000
Address: The Zone, Rosebank, Oxford Rd
Web: www.holidayinn.co.za.
Coordinates: 26° 8'49.81"S
28° 2'33.19"E (approximate).

Hyatt Regency Hotel. Phone: +27 11 280 1234. Address: 191 Oxford Road. Web: johannesburg.regency.hyatt.com. Coordinates: 26° 8'37.91"S, 28° 2'36.70"E.

Protea Hotel, Melrose Arch. ⓞⓞⓞⓞⓞ —
Phone: +27 11 214 6666
Address: 1 Melrose Square, Melrose Arch, Atholl Oaklands Road
Web: www.protea-melrosearch.co.za, www.africanpridehotels.com/melrose-arch-hotel.html. Coordinates: 26° 8'2.18"S, 28° 4'5.24"E.

Protea Hotel, Wanderers. ⓞⓞⓞⓞ — Phone: +27 11 770 5500. Address: Cnr Rudd Road and Corlett Drive. Web: www.proteahotels.com/protea-hotel-wanderers.html, www.protea-wanderers.co.za. Coordinates: 26° 8'3.35"S, 26° 8'3.35"S.

Ten Bompas. — Phone: +27 11 341 0282. Address: 10 Bompas Road, Dunkeld West, close to the British Consulate. Web: www.tenbompas.com. Coordinates: 26° 7'53.11"S, 28° 1'57.88"E

The Westcliff, Westcliff. ⓞⓞⓞⓞⓞ — Phone: +27 11 481 6000. Address: 67 Jan Smuts Avenue, Westcliff. Web: www.westcliff.co.za. Coordinates: 26°10'15.78"S, 28° 1'57.85"E. (Google Earth has some incorrect coordinates for this one).

Johannesburg Airport

City Lodge. — Phone: +27 11 552 7600. Address: Above the parkade, OR Tambo International Airport, Kempton Park. Web: http://www.citylodge.co.za/cl13.htm. Coordinates: 26° 7'57.50"S, 28°13'39.48"E.

D'Oreal Grande. ☺☺☺☺☺ — Phone: +27 0 11 928 1770. Address: 64 Jones Road/Street, Kempton Park. Web: http://www.doreale.com/emperorspalace/directions.asp. Coordinates: 26°8'39.90"E, 28°13'15.70"E

Holiday Inn Intercontinental. — Phone: +27 11 961 5400. Address: O.R. Tambo Airport. Web: www.holidayinn.co.za. Coordinates: 26° 7'57.50"S, 28°13'39.48"E

Metcourt Laurel Hotel. ☺☺☺ — Phone: +27 11 928 1928. Address: 64 Jones Road/Street, Kempton Park. Web: http://johannesburg.hotelguide.co.za/Johannesburg_Hotels-travel/johannesburg-hotel-metcourt-laurel-hotel-emperors.html. Coordinates: 26° 8'50.23"S, 28°13'25.26"E (approximate).

Southern Sun at OR Tambo. ☺☺☺☺☺ — Phone: +27 11 961 5400. Address: Airport Grounds, Jones Road, Kempton Park. Web: www.southernsun.com. Coordinates: 26° 8'10.94"S, 28°13'35.58"E

Soweto

The Soweto Hotel. — Phone:+ 27 11 527 7300. Address: Cnr Union Ave & Main Rd, The Walter Sisulu Square of Dedication, Kliptown, Soweto. Web: www.sowetohotel.co.za. Coordinates: 26°16'42.34"S, 27°53'21.46"E.

Bed and Breakfast Establishments

There are probably hundreds of these dotted around the city as well. I suggest you look at the following sites:

www.greatstaysa.co.za
www.johannesburg-guesthouses.co.za
www.bedandbreakfast.co.za

A small selection of Sandton-area B&Bs:

35 Oldensway. — My father-in-law's place. Affordable. A large 5-acre property with a pool, bar, and wifi, on M1 motorway. Phone: +27 11 802 1551. Address: 35 Oldensway, Kelvin, Sandton. Web: www.baikoff.co.za. Coordinates: 26° 4'19.47"S, 28° 5'24.72"E.

Elizabeth Manor Guest House. — Phone: +27 11 884 0880. Address: 141 1st Street /Elizabeth Street, Sandton. Web: elizabethmanor.co.za. Coordinates: 26° 6'22.14"S, 28° 2'39.21"E.

Rivonia Bed and Breakfast. ⊛⊛⊛⊛ — Phone: +27 11 803 2790. Address: 3 River Road (Entrance via 10 th Ave). Web: www.rivoniabb.co.za
Coordinates: 26° 3'1.66"S, 28° 3'55.01"E

Sandton Lodge. ⊛⊛⊛⊛ — They have three branches.
Web: www.sandtonlodge.co.za

Sandton Lodge Inanda
Address: 66, 6th Avenue, Inanda
Phone: + 27 11 788 4169, + 27 11 022 4169 | 021 5657
Coordinates: 26° 7'11.14"S, 28° 3'27.67"E

Sandton Lodge Bryanston
Address: 3 Davies Road, Bryanston
Phone: +27 11 463 2404
Coordinates: 26° 3'47.86"S, 28° 3'11.99"E

Sandton Lodge Rivonia
Address: 143 12th Avenue/ 13 River Road, cnr 12th Avenue & River Rd, Rivonia.
Phone: + 27 11 234-8713/4/5/6, + 27 11 022 4170/1
Coordinates: 26° 2'54.24"S, 28° 3'52.11"E

Tladi Lodge. ⊛⊛⊛⊛⊛ — Phone: +27 11 784 9240. Address: 16 David Street, Sandown. Web: www.tladilodge.co.za. Coordinates: 26° 5'31.32"S, 28° 4'3.10"E.

There are many more places; you simply need to search internet or ask Google Earth for "bed and breakfast" in the area that you want to stay.

Message to Hoteliers and Bed and Breakfast Owners

If you are a hotelier or bed and breakfast owner, and you wish to be listed in subsequent editions of this book, please contact me at *john@ostrowick.co.za.*

88

Chapter 14
Maps and Routes

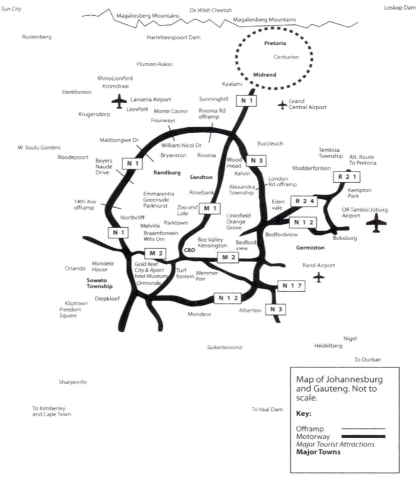

The map above is a conceptual map showing the layout of the major tourist attractions and towns mentioned in the book. The area shown is approximately 200km (East to West) x 150km (North to South). NB: Map is not to scale.

Recommended Day Trips

The following tourist attractions are near to each other, so it would make sense to go see them all on the same day or over two days if you happen to be staying in the area or wanting to see a number of attractions that are in the same area. Some of these attractions are quite far out from Johannesburg. So you may wonder why I listed them in my book on Johannesburg. The reason is that we Jo'burgers are so used to driving everywhere, and being stuck in traffic, that we don't consider a one or two hour drive to a tourist attraction to be a challenge, especially if there's a motorway all the way to the relevant tourist attraction.

The South

Group 1 — Ormonde: The Apartheid Museum, Gold Reef City, Soccer City.
Group 2 — Rosettenville/Turffontein: James Hall Transport Museum, Wemmer Pan, Santarama and Miniland.
Group 3 — Soweto: Mandela House Museum, Hector Pieterson Memorial, Freedom Square, Wandie's.

The Far South

Attraction 1 — Suikerbosrand Reserve.
Attraction 2 — Vaal Dam.
Attraction 3 — Sharpeville Memorial.

CBD

Group 1 — CBD: Carlton Centre, Johannesburg Art Gallery.
Group 2 — Newtown: Scibono Centre, Market Theatre, Gramadoelas, Mandela Bridge, MuseumAfrica. The Gauteng Tourism Bureau is directly opposite the square from MuseumAfrica.

Melville and Wits

Group 1 — Wits: The Planetarium, Origins Centre, Wits Theatre, Civic Theatre, Oriental Plaza at Fordsburg.
Group 2 — Melville: Restaurants, Melville Koppies (if open).

Greenside and Parkhurst

Group 1 — Parkhurst Restaurants.
Group 2 — Emmarentia Dam, Johannesburg Botanical Gardens, Greenside Restaurants.

Rosebank and Central

Group 1 — Rosebank Flea Market on a Sunday, Rosebank Mall and The Zone, Shops, art nouveau movies, restaurants.
Group 2 — Zoo Lake, the Zoo, the Military History Museum, Moyo's at the Zoo Lake. This might take two days.
Group 3 — Parktown North Restaurants.
Group 4 — Orange Grove and Norwood: Victory Theatre, Radium Beerhall or Grant Avenue Restaurants.

Sandton

Group 1 — Sandton City Mall, Nelson Mandela statue at the Square, Restaurants and shops. Library and Theatre on the Square. Art Gallery under the Library.
Group 2 — Village Walk and Blues Room at night. The stock exchange is now situated in Sandton.
Group 3 — Montecasino and Bird Park, Restaurants and Casino. Bryanston organic market is nearby.

East Rand

Group 1 — Eastgate Mall, Bruma Flea Market, Linksfield Ridge, George Harrison Statue, CCHQ nightclub.

90

Group 2 — Boksburg Flea Market, Plane watching at the nursery, Wild Waters Theme Park
Group 3 — Emperor's Palace Casino and Restaurants.

West

Group 1 — Walter Sisulu Botanical Gardens. Possibly Drive up Northcliff Ridge or go to dinner at Banbury Crossing on Malibongwe Drive; there might also be something on at the Dome.

Far North West

Group 1 — Sterkfontein and Maropeng. There is a hotel on-site so you can take your time. Cornuti in the Cradle is a good restaurant if you're not into meat. Or you might want to go to Carnivores.
Group 2 — Rhino Lion Park and Wonder Cave. There are chalets on-site so you can take your time.

Pretoria

Group 1 — Paul Kruger House and Church, Melrose House, Transvaal Museum, State Theatre, Union Buildings. This might take two days.
Group 2 — Pretoria Zoo. You'll need a whole day. They also do night tours.
Group 3 — Freedom Park, Voortrekker Monument.

Very Far North

Group 1 — Plumari Game Reserve and Hartebeespoort Dam, De Wildt Cheetah Centre. This will definitely take a few days.
Group 2 — Sun City. Give yourself at least two days. Pilanesburg Game Reserve nearby will take even longer.
Group 3 — Loskop Dam.

Navigation Hints

There are a number of major roads and routes that you can rely on to find your way around, and they all intersect. Please note that all the roads listed are two-way roads.

Note that there are a lot of "route markers" placed around the city. They are small blue or green signs with a route number and a direction (N/S/E/W). You can use these route markers to find your way around by looking for them in a South African mapbook, which you can get at any branch of CNA or PNA, or Exclusive Books in any mall.

I have provided some simple conceptual maps of Jo'burg's layout in this chapter; you should consult those maps while reading these descriptions.

Pay special attention to Jan Smuts Avenue as almost all the major tourist attractions north of the M2 are on it or near it.

The Ring Road: N1/N3/N12

The R24 motorway from the airport meets the ring road at Gillooley's interchange. This leads into the N12 (south), and the N3 (north). The N12 leads to Bedfordview, Alberton, Springs, Suikerbosrand, Nigel and Heidelberg, and eventually Durban (600km away!).

The N3 north goes past Linksfield Road, which leads to Orange Grove and Norwood, then Modderfontein Road, which leads to Highlands North and Rosebank. It then passes Alexandra Township (London Road), Marlboro Drive (Kelvin and Sandton CBD). It subsequently splits at Buccleuch (pronounced 'ba-**kloo**'). interchange. North takes you to Pretoria and Midrand, Roodepoort direction takes you west to Rivonia and Sunninghill (at first). **NB** — If you don't take the Roodepoort direction at the Buccleuch interchange, you will find yourself heading to Pretoria, and the soonest you can turn back is Allandale Road at Midrand.

If you continue west you pass the Rivonia offramp, then William Nicol (and Monte Casino), Malibongwe (where you can turn for the attractions in the far north-west), then Beyers Naudé, which also leads to the attractions in the far north-west. After Beyers Naudé is the 14th Avenue turnoff. I recommend that you take this rather than go further, as it gets tricky and you can end up going too far south.

If you carry on, you will get to Soweto. You should take the turn towards Ormonde/Aeroton unless you intend to go to Soweto. At this point you'll be on the Southern Bypass. Follow the Witbank and Pretoria signs west and north, and you'll eventually come back to Gillooley's interchange.

Major Roads Running North / South

Barry Hertzog. This starts at Empire Road just outside Milpark Hospital and travels north through Greenside and past Melville on the east. It ends in Linden/ Victory Park, where it feeds into 1st Avenue, Braam Fischer, and Malibongwe.

Beyers Naudé Drive, formerly known as DF Malan (in case someone refers to it by that name), which leads from the far north-west near Sterkfontein into Laser Park, Northgate Mall and the Coca Cola Dome, through to Randburg and Northcliff, and eventually Melville, where it becomes Main and University. At the end of Main is Campus Square mall and the University of Johannesburg.

Bowling Avenue. This runs from the Sandton CBD where it is called Katherine Street, to Sunninghill, more or less parallel to Rivonia Road. It changes to Bowling Avenue after Marlboro road.

Braam Fischer Drive (formerly HF Verwoerd), starts in Linden/Victory Park and travels north through Randburg and Bryanston. It meets with William Nicol, by which time it has changed its name to Main. It eventually crosses the ring road and enters Fourways/ Magaliessig, where Monte Casino can be found.

The Golden Highway. This splits off the M2 (the south part of the ring road) and runs south past Gold Reef City, the Apartheid Museum, and then past Diepkloof in Soweto.

Jan Smuts Avenue. This splits at Hyde Park and becomes William Nicol Drive. The split to the east is William Nicol, the split to the west stays Jan Smuts and leads to Randburg CBD. Jan Smuts/ William Nicol has the following tourist attractions on it, from north to south: Monte Casino (as William Nicol), Sandton City, Hyde Park Mall, (Changes to Jan Smuts here), Rosebank, The Zoo, Zoo Lake and the Military History Museum. It continues to Wits University and its museums and Planetarium, changes to Bertha Street, becomes the Nelson Mandela Bridge, then enters Newtown and the CBD. Probably the most important road for a tourist.

Katherine St — See Bowling Avenue.

Louis Botha Avenue. This starts at Hillbrow in the CBD, near Wits University and Empire Road, passes Norwood where Grant Avenue restaurants lie, passes Alexandra Township and

Wynberg industrial area, at which point it becomes the Old Pretoria road and passes Kelvin and Woodmead. The Hillbrow Tower, St Johns College, King Edwards, Victory Theatre, Norwood, routes to Rosebank, and the Radium Beer Hall are all accessible via Louis Botha.

The M1 Motorway, which starts at Empire Road near Wits University, passes the Glenhove offramp which leads to Rosebank (west) and Norwood (east), passes Corlett Drive which leads to Hyde Park and Illovo, and Wanderers Cricket Stadium (west), just near Oxford Road. The M1 proceeds north-east and passes the Grayston offramp, which leads to the Sandton CBD, and then the Marlboro offramp, which leads (south west via Katherine) to the Sandton CBD, or north west via South Road to Rivonia. If you ignore the Marlboro offramp, the next offramp is Woodmead, which leads you to Woodmead, Sunninghill and Rivonia. After Woodmead, the M1 leads into the N1 to Roodepoort, which takes you onto the ring road west-bound.

Malibongwe Drive, formerly known as Hans Strydom (just in case someone calls it that), leads from the far north-west near Sterkfontein all the way to Randburg and then Greenside.

Oxford Road — see Rivonia Road.

Rivonia Road. This starts as Oxford Road at Wits University Education Campus, splitting into 1st at Killarney (ahead of you) and Oxford to the left. It becomes Rivonia Road at Sandton. It has Rosebank, the Military History Museum, Hyde Park, Illovo Thrupps Shopping Centre, and Sandton City on it. If you follow it all the way to Rivonia, many shops and restaurants can be found

along the way. It eventually crosses the ring road and enters Sunninghill and Witkoppen Road, which are just south of Kyalami and Midrand.

William Nicol — see Jan Smuts.

Major Roads Running East / West

Corlett Drive. This runs from Kew/ Lyndhurst/Alexandra Township in the east, over Louis Botha, through Bramley, into Oxford Road near Hyde Park. The Wanderers Cricket Stadium is on Corlett.

Empire Road. This runs from the Northcliff/Quellerina/Florida area in the west (where it is first Ontdekkers Rd). It becomes Perth Road outside Back2Basix, Westdene, Sophiatown and the University of Johannesburg. When it gets to Melville it becomes Stanley Rd. It becomes Empire Rd outside Wits University and the Milpark Hospital. After Wits it proceeds into Hillbrow and meets up with Louis Botha Avenue.

Grayston Drive. This leads from the Sandton CBD and suburbs to the M1 central motorway. It cuts through Katherine Road. Your best route to the M1 motorway from Sandton CBD. Watch out for window washers on the bridge.

Kitchener Avenue. This road runs directly from the R24 from the airport straight into the heart of the Jo'burg CBD via Bez Valley. Just before you enter the city you will cross Bertrams Road. If you turn right there, it will take you almost immediately to Ellis Park Stadium and Hillbrow (very dodgy, avoid!).

Main Reef Road. This runs from Randfontein and Kagiso Township in the west, across past the top of Soweto, through the lower end of the city (Selby) after crossing the ring road. It runs all the way across the south of Jo'burg.

Marlboro Drive/South Road. Leading away from Sandton's Rivonia Road in the CBD, down a steep hill, South Road feeds into Katherine/Bowling and meets up with Marlboro Drive, which skims between Kelvin and Alexandra Township, eventually leading to the N3/N12 ring road. If you turn north on the ring road, you'll head towards Sunninghill and Rivonia again, if you turn south, you will head towards Modderfontein, Edenvale, and the airport. This is your key route out of Sandton to the airport.

Modderfontein Road. This runs from Modderfontein and Tembisa Township past Edenvale and the ring road, then past the Edenvale hospital. At this point you can turn right into Johannesburg Road, which takes you to Louis Botha Drive and Highlands North, and eventually Rosebank, or, you can carry on. It eventually takes you through Sandringham, into Orange Grove, and eventually, Louis Botha Avenue and Norwood.

Republic Road. This runs in an arc from William Nicol in Sandton, then runs through over Jan Smuts Avenue, then west past the Brightwater Commons mall (which has many restaurants, a park and flea market), then curves south through Fontainebleau, Randpark, Windsor, Cresta (where there's another big mall). It ends in Linden near Greenside, where it becomes 3rd Ave.

Roberts Avenue. This runs parallel to Kitchener through Kensington (note there is a *Kensington B* in Randburg, which has nothing to do with this Kensington). Roberts Ave starts at the curve near Eastgate Shopping Centre/Park Meadows Mall and runs all the way into the city centre. Jeppe Boys High school, Abyssinia and Adega Restaurants are on this road.

Sandton Drive. This joins William Nicol and Rivonia Road, and passes Sandton City Mall.

Tana Road. This runs from Linden past the top of Greenside (where the Emmarentia Dam and Botanical gardens can be found), into Parktown North where it becomes 7th avenue, where the restaurants are. If you follow it further, it ends in Jan Smuts avenue just west of Rosebank Mall. There is a small "Tana" road in Sunninghill. It is unrelated to this one. Tana starts as Preller, off Beyers Naudé, becomes Hofmeyer, Tana, Victory, 6th, 7th (west to east).

Witkoppen Road, which partly circumnavigates the north-west of the city, lies further north than the ring road. It passes from Roodepoort, where it's called Christiaan De Wet and then Northumberland. It goes all the way to Fourways (where Monte Casino is), and Sunninghill (across the ring road from Rivonia). It becomes Witkoppen when it crosses Malibongwe Drive.

NB: The maps on the following pages do not show thousands of side roads and less important roads; they only show the key roads that you need to know in order to navigate around the city. They also do not show anything south of the M2. I strongly recommend that you purchase a proper map book, or bring a GPS, when coming to Johannesburg — the inhabited area and adjoining towns, excluding Pretoria, are 70km across and 50km top-to-bottom.

94

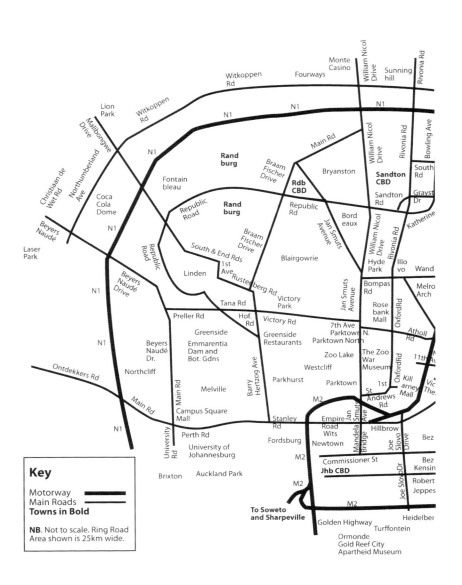

Conceptual Map (not to scale) — West side of Johannesburg.

95

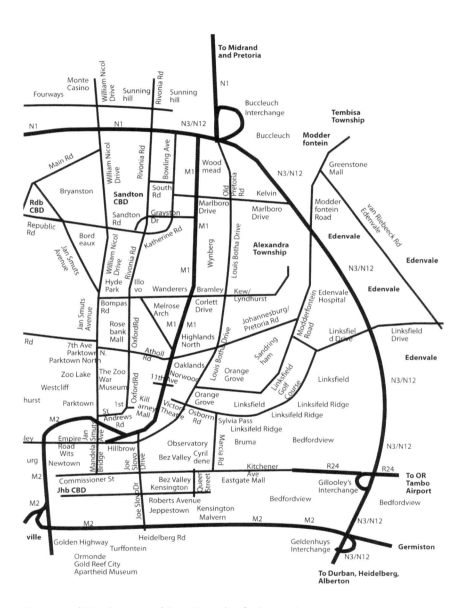

Conceptual Map (not to scale) — East side of Johannesburg.

Printed in Great Britain
by Amazon.co.uk, Ltd.,
Marston Gate.